Translation and Multilingual Natural Language Processing

Chief Editor: Oliver Czulo (Universität Leipzig)
Consulting Editors: Silvia Hansen-Schirra (Johannes Gutenberg-Universität Mainz), Reinhard Rapp (Johannes Gutenberg-Universität Mainz)

In this series:

1. Fantinuoli, Claudio & Federico Zanettin (eds.). New directions in corpus-based translation studies.

2. Hansen-Schirra, Silvia & Sambor Grucza (eds.). Eyetracking and Applied Linguistics.

3. Neumann, Stella, Oliver Čulo & Silvia Hansen-Schirra (eds.). Annotation, exploitation and evaluation of parallel corpora: TC3 I.

4. Čulo, Oliver & Silvia Hansen-Schirra (eds.). Crossroads between Contrastive Linguistics, Translation Studies and Machine Translation: TC3 II.

5. Rehm, Georg, Felix Sasaki, Daniel Stein & Andreas Witt (eds.). Language technologies for a multilingual Europe: TC3 III.

6. Menzel, Katrin, Ekaterina Lapshinova-Koltunski & Kerstin Anna Kunz (eds.). New perspectives on cohesion and coherence: Implications for translation.

ISSN: 2364-8899

New perspectives on cohesion and coherence

Implications for translation

Edited by

Katrin Menzel

Ekaterina Lapshinova-Koltunski

Kerstin Kunz

Katrin Menzel, Ekaterina Lapshinova-Koltunski & Kerstin Kunz (eds.). 2017.
New perspectives on cohesion and coherence: Implications for translation
(Translation and Multilingual Natural Language Processing 6). Berlin: Language Science Press.

This title can be downloaded at:
http://langsci-press.org/catalog/book/107
© 2017, the authors
Published under the Creative Commons Attribution 4.0 Licence (CC BY 4.0):
http://creativecommons.org/licenses/by/4.0/
ISBN: 978-3-946234-72-2 (Digital)
      978-3-946234-80-7 (Hardcover)
      978-3-946234-84-5 (Softcover)
ISSN: 2364-8899
DOI:10.5281/zenodo.814452

Cover and concept of design: Ulrike Harbort
Typesetting: Felix Kopecky, Sebastian Nordhoff, Iana Stefanova
Proofreading: Alec Shaw, Alessia Battisti, Ahmet Bilal Özdemir, Anca Gâță, Andreea Calude, Bev Erasmus, Brett Reynolds, Christian Döhler, Claudia Marzi, Dominik Lukes, Gabrielle Hodge, Ikmi Nur Oktavianti, Jean Nitzke, Mario Bisiada, Martin Hilpert, Timm Lichte, Viola Wiegand
Fonts: Linux Libertine, Arimo, DejaVu Sans Mono
Typesetting software: X∃LATEX

Language Science Press
Habelschwerdter Allee 45
14195 Berlin, Germany
langsci-press.org
Storage and cataloguing done by FU Berlin

Language Science Press has no responsibility for the persistence or accuracy of URLs for external or third-party Internet websites referred to in this publication, and does not guarantee that any content on such websites is, or will remain, accurate or appropriate.

Contents

1 Cohesion and coherence in multilingual contexts
  Katrin Menzel, Ekaterina Lapshinova-Koltunski & Kerstin Kunz   1

2 Discourse connectives: From historical origin to present-day development
  Magdaléna Rysová   11

3 Possibilities of text coherence analysis in the Prague Dependency Treebank
  Kateřina Rysová   35

4 Applying computer-assisted coreferential analysis to a study of terminological variation in multilingual parallel corpora
  Koen Kerremans   49

5 Testing target text fluency: A machine learning approach to detecting syntactic translationese in English-Russian translation
  Maria Kunilovskaya & Andrey Kutuzov   75

6 Cohesion and translation variation: Corpus-based analysis of translation varieties
  Ekaterina Lapshinova-Koltunski   105

7 Examining lexical coherence in a multilingual setting
  Karin Sim Smith & Lucia Specia   131

Indexes   151

Chapter 1

Cohesion and coherence in multilingual contexts

Katrin Menzel
Saarland University

Ekaterina Lapshinova-Koltunski
Saarland University

Kerstin Kunz
Heidelberg University

1 Introduction

The volume will investigate textual relations of cohesion and coherence in translation and multilingual text production with a strong focus on innovative methods of empirical analysis as well as technology and computation. Given the amount of multilingual computation that is taking place, this topic is important for both human and machine translation and further multilingual studies.

Coherence and cohesion, the two concepts addressed by the papers in this book, are closely connected and are sometimes even regarded as synonymous (see e.g. Brinker 2010). We draw a distinction concerning the realization by linguistic means.

COHERENCE first of all is a cognitive phenomenon. Its recognition is rather subjective as it involves text- and reader-based features and refers to the logical flow of interrelated topics (or experiential domains) in a text, thus establishing a mental textual world. COHESION can be regarded as an explicit indicator of relations between topics in a text. It refers to the text-internal relationship of linguistic elements that are overtly linked via lexical and grammatical devices across sentence boundaries. The main types of cohesion generally stated in the literature are coreference, substitution/ ellipsis, conjunction and lexical cohesion (Halliday & Hasan (1976)). They create relations of identity or comparison, logico-semantic relations or similarity. In the case of coreference and lexical cohesion, COHESIVE CHAINS may contain two or more elements and may span local or global stretches of a text (Halliday & Hasan 1976; Widdowson 1979).

There is another linguistic phenomenon dealt with in several studies of this book, which interacts with cohesion and which also contributes to the overall coherence and topic continuity of a text: INFORMATION STRUCTURE concerns the linguistic marking of textual information as new/ relevant/ salient or old/ less relevant/ less salient (Krifka 2007; Lambrecht 1994). The information in question is presented through linear arrangement of syntactic constituents as either theme or theme, topic or focus or, more generally speaking, in sentence-initial or sentence-final position.

Hence, coherence may or may not be signaled by linguistic markers at the text surface, while cohesion and information structure are explicit linguistic strategies which enhance the recognition of conceptual continuity and the logical flow of topics in texts (Louwerse & Graesser 2007; Halliday & Matthiessen 2004).

One major task involved in the process of translation is to identify the linguistic triggers employed in the source text to develop, relate and change topics. Moreover, the conceptual relations in the mental textual world have to be transferred into the target text by using strategies of cohesion and information structure that conform to target-language conventions. Empirical knowledge about language contrasts in the use of these explicit means and about adequate/ preferred translation strategies is one essential key to systematize the logical flow of topics in human and machine translation. The aim of this volume is to bring together scholars analyzing the cohesion and information structure from different research perspectives that cover translation-relevant topics: language contrast, translationese and machine translation. What these approaches share is that they investigate instantiations of discourse phenomena in multilingual contexts. Moreover, language comparison in the contributions of this volume is based on empirical data. The challenges here can be identified with respect to the following methodological questions:

1. What is the best way to arrive at a cost-effective operationalization of the annotation process when dealing with a broader range of discourse phenomena?

2. Which statistical techniques are needed and are adequate for the analysis? And which methods can be combined for data interpretation?

3. Which applications of the knowledge acquired are possible in multilingual computation, especially in machine translation?

The contributions of different scholars and research groups involved in our volume reflect these questions. All contributions have undergone a rigorous double blind peer reviewing process, each being assessed by two external reviewers. On the one hand, some contributions will concentrate on procedures to analyse cohesion and coherence from a corpus-linguistic perspective (M. Rysová; K. Rysová). On the other hand, our volume will include papers with a particular focus on textual cohesion in parallel corpora that include both originals and translated texts (Kerremans; Kutuzov, Kunilovskaya). Finally, the papers in the volume will also include discussions on the nature of cohesion and coherence with implications for human and machine translation (Lapshinova-Koltunski; Sim Smith, Specia).

Targeting the questions raised above and addressing them together from different research angles, the present volume will contribute to moving empirical translation studies ahead.

2 Phenomena under analysis: Cohesion and coherence

What unifies all of the studies gathered in this volume is that they deal with explicit means of coherence: some works are concerned with particular types of cohesion (M. Rysová; Lapshinova-Koltunski; Sim Smith, Specia), some of them look into the interplay of these different types (Kerremans; Lapshinova-Koltunksi), and some investigate their interaction with information structure (K. Rysová; Kunilovskaya, Kutuzov; Sim Smith, Specia) In most studies, the focus is on the cohesive devices triggering a cohesive relation (M. Rysová; Lapshinova-Koltunski; Kunilovskaya, Kutuzov), others also take account of the relations between cohesive elements (K. Rysová; Kerremans; Sim Smith, Specia).

M. Rysová considers discourse connectives from an etymological perspective in order to set up a structural classification of different connective types for her corpus-linguistic analysis of the Prague Discourse Treebank. Taking account of their degree of grammaticalization, she draws a main distinction between primary and secondary discourse connectives. While both types share their textual function of signaling logico-semantic relations between different textual passages (clauses, clause complexes and larger chunks), they differ in terms of their internal structure as well as their syntactic function.

K. Rysová looks into the interplay of coreference and information structure. She analyses whether different types of coreferential expressions occur in the topic or the focus of a sentence. More precisely, coreferential anaphors or antecedents may collide with syntactic elements that are non-contrastive contextually bound (typically given information), contrastive contextually bound (information on some alternative that can be derived from the context but may not be explicitly given), or non-contextually bound (textually new information).

Kerremans focuses on the interaction of coreference and lexical cohesion in order to determine terminological variants of the same conceptual entity. He groups all nominal elements referring to the same entity in coreference chains and merges these chains with corresponding chains in other texts of the same language. Assigning the coreference chains in the English source texts to the corresponding chains in the Dutch and French target texts eventually permits enriching a terminological database.

Kunilovskaya, Kutuzov consider the mapping of given and new information onto syntactic structure. They train machine learning models to compare originals and translations in terms of (a-) typical patterns at sentence boundaries. For this purpose, they analyze a set of cohesive devices (e.g. pronouns and conjunctions) and other features (e.g. parts of speech, word length) in Russian translations from English and in Russian original texts. Contrasts are identified in terms of where and in which linear order these features occur before and after sentence starts.

Lapshinova compares the distribution of various types of cohesion in human and machine translation. Her focus is on cohesive devices indicating identity of reference (coreference) and logico-semantic relations (conjunction). Within coreference, she distinguishes devices serving as nominal heads (e.g. personal and demonstrative pronouns) and those functioning as modifiers (e.g. the definite article, demonstrative determiners). Conjunctions are classified in terms of their syntactic function (e.g. subordinating or coordinating conjunction and the logico-semantic relation they indicate (e.g. additive or temporal). Translations from English into German and original texts of the two languages.

Sim Smith, Specia investigate the textual distribution of lexical cohesion for improving statistical machine translation. They apply two statistical techniques in order to assess the lexical coherence of texts in a multilingual parallel corpus (English, French and German). Contrasts between languages and between translations and originals are identified by analyzing nominal elements contained in lexical chains of one and the same document. The criteria of comparison included in the research are a) in which sentences these elements appear and b) in which syntactic function (subject vs. other).

3 Corpora and languages

This volume has much to offer to the reader interested in electronic corpora as language resources. It provides information on current research into textual characteristics and discourse structures in different types of language corpora and suggests solutions to questions related to annotation procedures, the quantitative analysis and interpretation of data and machine translation for various languages.

Several types of corpora were used for the studies in this volume. Some contributions focus on large-scale monolingual corpora with the purpose of analyzing a particular language and developing methods that can be applied to other languages as well where similar corpora are available. Some researchers demonstrate the pedagogical and scientific value of native and learner corpora that help to reveal differences between native speakers of a given language and non-native speakers in their ways of creating textuality. Finally, some contributions use bi- or multilingual parallel or comparable corpora consisting either of texts in a language and their translations in another language or of original texts in several languages that are similar with regard to their sampling frame, balance and representativeness.

The annotation of discourse relations and the frequency of discourse connectives in large monolingual corpora such as the the Prague Discourse Treebank 2.0 (PDiT) consisting of Czech newspaper texts as a particular type of written texts are discussed in the chapter by M. Rysová. She examines the historical origin of prototypical discourse connectives in Czech, English and German and demonstrates how these findings can help translators to produce more accurate translations of connectives in these languages. Furthermore, her observations are helpful for the annotation of connectives in large corpora of these languages. Discourse connectives arose from various parts of speech in Czech, English and German and display different stages of grammaticalization. In corpus data for modern stages of the languages investigated in this chapter, they can occur, for instance, in the form of conjunctions, particles, prepositional phrases or fixed collocations. Her chapter provides an angle to address such challenges to annotators of discourse connectives as groups of expressions that may not seem straightforward to define in various languages.

K. Rysová's chapter also addresses the analysis of texts from the Prague Dependency Treebank as a large monolingual corpus and focuses on coreferential relations and information structure in Czech. Her chapter demonstrates that the complexity of text coherence demands extensive language resources of authentic texts from a given language. Large monolingual corpora with multilayer annotation are still relatively rare for many languages. K. Rysová's analysis encourages research into other languages and recommends applying the methodology she used for the annotation and analysis of coreferential relation and information structure to other languages for which similar resources exist.

Kerremans' chapter demonstrates the invaluable contribution of multilingual parallel corpora including both originals and translated texts as a resource for comparative linguistics and translation studies. The corpus created for Kerremans' study is comprised of written English original texts and their translations into French and Dutch. Terminological variants and coreferential relations from the English source texts have been analyzed from a contrastive perspective. The translation equivalents of these phenomena were retrieved from the French and Dutch target texts in order to create a useful terminological database of translation units and their target-language equivalents for the English-French and the English-Dutch language pairs.

The chapter by Kunilovskaya, Kutuzov deals with the benefits which can be gained from the conjoined use of native and learner corpus data. It compares native and learner varieties of the Russian language with regard to the use of sentence boundaries in a subcorpus of mass media texts from the Russian Learner Translator Corpus. The corpus includes English-Russian learner translations and a genre-comparable subcorpus of the Russian National Corpus, aiming at uncovering differences between native Russian and its learner translated variant.

The chapter by Sim Smith, Specia provides a compelling example of how multilingual corpus data can be used to improve the translation quality in machine-translation models. In this study, original and translated news excerpts in English, French and German from a parallel corpus from the Workshop on Statistical Machine Translation (WMT) were used as well as translations of from French into English from the LIG corpus, which contains news excerpts drawn from various WMT years. The translations that were used for the analysis were provided by human professional translators. They were analyzed with regard to the realisation of lexical coherence, and a multilingual comparative entity-based grid was developed that consists of various types of documents covering the three languages under comparison.

The chapter by Lapshinova-Koltunski describes innovative corpus-based methods to analyze the frequencies and distributions of cohesive devices in multilingual data. Her bilingual corpus contains comparable English and German data for various written text types as well as multiple translations into German which were produced by human translators with different levels of expertise and by different machine translation systems. This contribution has its focus on the analysis of cohesion in texts from different languages which vary along dimensions such as text-production type, translation method involved and systemic contrasts between source and target language.

4 Methods of investigation

The contributions to this volume cover a wide range of different methods of analysis, starting from manual investigation of previously annotated data, across semi-automatic procedures supporting manual analysis towards fully computational approaches such as entity-grid calculation and automatic sentence segmentation with machine-learning techniques.

Annotation of corpora with information on cohesion- or coherence-related phenomena play a significant role in various descriptive studies based on corpora. They receive particular attention in chapters 2, 3 and 4, in which research design relies to a large extent on annotation. In chapters 5, 6 and partly 7, automatic procedures are used to identify cohesion and coherence phenomena.

Issues of annotation of explicit discourse relations (i.e. relations expressed by concrete language means) in the PDiT are addressed in the study by M. Rysová. She uses the data from PDiT for her analysis to illustrate the difficulty of delineating the boundaries between connectives and non-connectives. For instance, she discusses if frozen lexical forms are a sufficient argument for excluding multiword phrases from discourse connectives and their annotation in the corpus. These phrases clearly signal discourse relations within a text, but they significantly differ from the "prototypical", lexical connectives. The author provides an analysis of historical formation of discourse connectives, justifying their claim that discourse connectives are not a closed class of expressions but rather a scale mapping the grammaticalization of the individual connective expressions. The author believes that this justification may help with the annotation of discourse in large corpora, as was done for PDiT.

The Prague Dependency Treebank was used in the analyses by K. Rysová, who demonstrates how different annotation layers can be used to examine text coherence. The author concentrates on the interplay of two annotation layers: text coreference and sentence information structure. The annotation of sentence information structure is related to contextual boundness, whereas text coreference is understood as the use of different language means for marking the same object of textual reference (the antecedent and the anaphor referents are identical). The author defines all mutual possibilities of coreference relations among contextually bound and contextually non-bound sentence items, and analyzes their corpus occurrences. The client-server PML Tree Query (Štěpánek & Pajas 2010) was used to extract the frequency information. The client part is an extension of the tree editor TrEd2 (Pajas & Štěpánek 2008). K. Rysová analyzes the proportion of various mutual possibilities on the basis of corpus occurrences in PDT.

Kerremans uses coreference analysis to study inter- and intralingual terminology variation in a parallel corpus. He proposes a semi-automatic method to annotate terminological patterns that belong to the same coreference chain (called coreferential terminological variants) as an alternative to fully manual labeling, which turns out to be a labour-intensive process. Kerremans method is aimed at supporting manual identification of coreferential terminological variants in the English source texts, annotating these variants according to a common cluster label, extracting them from the text and storing them in a separate database. The automated procedures are implemented in a Perl script ensuring completeness, accuracy and consistency in the data obtained.

Kunilovskaya, Kutuzov also apply semi-automatic procedures to a multilingual corpus that contains both parallel and comparable texts. These semi-automatic procedures are applied to detect divergences in sentence structures between translations into Russian and Russian non-translations. The authors deploy statistical techniques from machine learning: they train a decision-tree model to describe the contextual features of sentence boundaries in the reference corpus of Russian texts, which are considered to be an approximation of the standard language variety. The model is then applied to the translation learner corpus, and translated sentences that are different from the standard language variety are identified through the evaluation of predictors and their combinations. Kunilovskaya, Kutuzov use a number of contextual features in sentence-boundary environments for evaluation. The initial set of 82 features was reduced to 48 with the help of feature selection procedures, allowing them to keep only predictive ones. The results of their analysis permit, on the one hand, to manually inspect cases of the model failing to predict sentence boundaries and possibly find the route causes, and on the other hand, to train another model which predicts not sentence boundaries, but inconsistencies between the first-model decisions and what a translator did in a particular context.

Sim Smith, Specia perform an exploratory analysis of lexical coherence in a multilingual context with a view to identifying patterns that could later be used to improve overall translation quality in machine translation models. They use an entity-grid model and an entity-graph metric – two entity-based frameworks that have previously been used for assessing coherence in a monolingual setting.

The authors try to understand how lexical coherence is realized across different languages and apply these techniques in a multilingual setting for the first time. The entity-grid approach is applied to a parallel corpus. Simply tracking the existence or absence of entities allows for direct comparison across languages. However, entity transition patterns may vary from language to language, while retaining an overall degree of coherence. In order to illustrate the differences between the distributions of entity transitions over the different languages, the authors compute divergence scores. They also analyze the reasons for the observed divergence by taking a closer look at their data.

Lapshinova-Koltunski uses a number of visualisation and statistical techniques to investigate the distributional characteristics of subcorpora in terms of occurrences of cohesive devices in human and machine translation. The cohesive features chosen for the comparative analysis were obtained on the basis of automatic linguistic annotation: tokenisation, lemmatisation, part-of-speech tags and segmentation into syntactic chunks and sentences. Cohesive features are operationalized with the Corpus Query Processor (CQP) queries (Evert 2010). This tool allows definition of language patterns in the form of regular expressions that can integrate string, part-of-speech and chunk tags, as well as further constraints, e.g. position in a sentence. With the help of CQP queries, frequencies of various cohesive features are extracted from a corpus containing translation varieties. Then, various descriptive techniques are used to observe and explore differences between groups of texts and subcorpora under analysis.

5 Conclusion

The contributors to this volume are experts on discourse phenomena and textuality who address these issues from an empirical perspective. We hope that this volume provides an innovative and useful contribution to the advancement of linguistic theory and discourse-oriented corpus studies. This volume also aims at addressing the challenges for human and machine translation arising from the interplay of grammatical and lexical indicators of textual cohesion and coherence.

The chapters in this volume are written in an accessible style. They epitomize the latest research, thus making this book useful to both experts of discourse studies and computational linguistics, as well as advanced students with an interest in these disciplines. We hope that this volume will serve as a catalyst to other researchers and will facilitate further advances in the development of cost-effective annotation procedures, in the application of statistical techniques for the analysis of linguistic phenomena, the elaboration of new methods for data interpretation in multilingual corpus linguistics and machine translation.

References

Brinker, Klaus. 2010. *Linguistische Textanalyse: Eine Einführung in Grundbegriffe und Methoden*. 7th edn. Berlin: Erich Schmidt Verlag.

Evert, Stefan. 2010. *The IMS Open Corpus Workbench (CWB) CQP Query Language Tutorial*. Version CWB Version 3.0. The OCWB Development Team. http://cwb.sourceforge.net/.

Halliday, Michael A. K. & Ruqaiya Hasan. 1976. *Cohesion in English*. London: Longman Publishing.

Halliday, Michael A. K. & Christian Matthiessen. 2004. *Introduction to functional grammar*. 3rd edition. London: Arnold.

Krifka, Manfred. 2007. Basic notions of information structure. In Caroline Fery & Manfred Krifka (eds.), *Interdisciplinary studies of information structure 6*, 13–56. Potsdam: Universitätsverlag.

Lambrecht, Knud. 1994. *Information structure and sentence form: Topic, focus, and the mental representations of discourse referents*. Cambridge: Cambridge University Press.

Louwerse, Max M. & Arthur C. Graesser. 2007. Coherence in discourse. In P. Strazny (ed.), *Encyclopedia of linguistics*, 216–218. Chicago: Fitzroy Dearborn.

Pajas, Petr & Jan Štěpánek. 2008. Recent advances in a Feature-Rich framework for treebank annotation. In Donia Scott & Hans Uszkoreit (eds.), *The 22nd international Conference on Computational Linguistics - Proceedings of the Conference*, vol. 2, 673–680. Manchester, UK: The Coling 2008 Organizing Committee.

Štěpánek, Jan & Petr Pajas. 2010. Querying diverse treebanks in a uniform way. In *Proceedings of the 7th International Conference on Language Resources and Evaluation (LREC 2010)*, 1828–1835. Valletta, Malta: European Language Resources Association.

Widdowson, H. G. 1979. *Explorations in applied linguistics*. Oxford: Oxford University Press.

Chapter 2

Discourse connectives: From historical origin to present-day development

Magdaléna Rysová
Charles University, Faculty of Mathematics and Physics

> The paper focuses on the description and delimitation of discourse connectives, i.e. linguistic expressions significantly contributing to text coherence and generally helping the reader to better understand semantic relations within a text. The paper discusses the historical origin of discourse connectives viewed from the perspective of present-day linguistics. Its aim is to define present-day discourse connectives according to their historical origin through which we see what is happening in discourse in contemporary language. The paper analyzes the historical origin of the most frequent connectives in Czech, English and German (which could be useful for more accurate translations of connectives in these languages) and point out that they underwent a similar process to gain a status of present-day discourse connectives. The paper argues that this historical origin or process of rising discourse connectives might be language universal. Finally, the paper demonstrates how these observations may be helpful for annotations of discourse in large corpora.

1 Introduction and motivation

Currently, linguistic research focuses often on creating and analyzing big language data. One of the frequently discussed topics of corpus linguistics is the annotation of discourse carried out especially through detection of discourse connectives. However, discourse connectives are not an easily definable group of expressions. Linguistic means signaling discourse relations may be conjunctions like *but, or* etc., prepositional phrases like *for this reason*, fixed collocations like

Magdaléna Rysová. 2017. Discourse connectives: From historical origin to present-day development. In Katrin Menzel, Ekaterina Lapshinova-Koltunski & Kerstin Kunz (eds.), *New perspectives on cohesion and coherence*, 11–32. Berlin: Language Science Press. DOI:10.5281/zenodo.814460

as seen, simply speaking etc., i.e. expressions with a different degree of lexicalization, syntactic integration or grammaticalization. Therefore, the paper concentrates on formulating clear boundaries of discourse connectives based on a deep linguistic research.

The paper analyzes the historical origin of the most frequent present-day connectives (mainly in Czech in comparison to other languages like English and German) to observe their tendencies or typical behaviour from a diachronic point of view, which may help us in annotation of connectives in large corpora (mainly in answering the question where to state the boundaries between connectives and non-connectives that could significantly facilitate the decision which expressions to capture in the annotation and which not). In other words, the paper tries to answer what we can learn from discourse connective formation and historical development and what this may tell us about present-day structuring of discourse.

The need for a clearly defined category of discourse connectives in Czech arose mainly during the annotation of discourse relations in the Prague Discourse Treebank (PDiT) pointing out several problematic issues. One of the most crucial was where and according to which general criteria to state the boundaries between connectives and non-connectives as well as between explicitness and implicitness of discourse relations. An explicit discourse relation is usually defined as a relation between two segments of text that is signaled by a particular language expression (discourse connective), typically by conjunctions like *a* 'and', *ale* 'but', *nebo* 'or' etc. However, during the annotations, we had to deal with examples of clear discourse relations expressed by explicit language means that, however, significantly differed from those typical examples of connectives. Such means included multiword phrases often having the function of sentence elements (like *kvůli tomu* 'due to this', *z tohoto důvodu* 'for this reason', *hlavní podmínkou bylo* 'the main condition was', *stejným dechem* 'in the same breath' etc.). Therefore, it was necessary to answer the question whether such expressions may be also considered discourse connectives and therefore included into the annotation of the PDiT or not.

It appeared that it is very helpful to look for the answer in the historical origin of the present-day typical connectives, i.e. expressions that would be without doubt classified as discourse connectives by most of the authors (like the mentioned conjunctions *a* 'and', *ale* 'but', *nebo* 'or' and many others). The results of such research (combined with the analysis of the present-day corpus data) are presented in this paper.

2 Theoretical discussions on discourse connectives

Discourse connectives are in various linguistic approaches defined very differently, which is mainly due to their complexity and hardly definable boundaries. There are several definitions highlighting different language aspects of discourse connectives – concerning their part-of-speech membership, lexical stability, phonological behaviour, position in the sentence etc. Most of the authors agree on defining the prototypical examples of connectives, i.e. expressions like *but, while, when, because* etc. and differ especially in multiword collocations like *for this reason, generally speaking* etc. The prototypical connectives are usually defined as monomorphemic, prosodically independent, phonologically short or reduced words (see Zwicky 1985; Urgelles-Coll 2010) that are syntactically separated from the rest of the sentence (see Schiffrin 1987; Zwicky 1985), not integrated into the clause structure (see Urgelles-Coll 2010) and that usually occupy the first position in the sentence (see Schiffrin 1987; Zwicky 1985; Schourup 1999; Fischer 2006).

Considering part-of-speech membership, some authors classify connectives as conjunctions (both subordinating and coordinating), prepositional phrases and adverbs (see Prasad et al. 2008; Prasad, Joshi & Webber 2010), others also as particles and nominal phrases (see Hansen 1998; Aijmer 2002), others include also some types of idioms (like *all things considered*, see Fraser 1999).

However, some of the mentioned syntactic classes (like prepositional phrases or nominal phrases) do not correspond to the definitions of discourse connectives stated above, i.e., for example, that connectives are usually short, not integrated into clause structure etc. Some of the authors define discourse connectives in a narrow sense (see e.g. Shloush 1998; Hakulinen 1998; Maschler 2000 who limit connectives only to synsemantic, i.e. grammatical words), some in a broader sense (e.g. according to Schiffrin 1987, discourse relations may be realized even through paralinguistic features and non-verbal gestures).

This paper contributes to these discussions on discourse connectives and looks at them from the diachronic point of view. It argues that the historical development of discourse connectives may point out many things about general tendencies in present-day structuring of discourse.

3 Methods and material

The analysis of discourse connectives in Czech is carried out on the data of the Prague Discourse Treebank 2.0 (PDiT; Rysová et al. 2016), i.e. on almost 50 thousand annotated sentences from Czech newspaper texts. The PDiT is a multilayer annotated corpus containing annotation on three levels at once: the morphological level, the surface syntactic level (called analytical) and the deep syntactico-semantic level (called tectogrammatic). At the same time, the PDiT texts are enriched by the annotation of sentence information structure[1] and various discourse phenomena like coreference and anaphora and especially by the annotation of explicit discourse relations (i.e. relations expressed by concrete language means, not implicitly).

The annotation of discourse relations in the PDiT (based on a detection of discourse connectives within a text) does not use any pre-defined list of discourse connectives (as some similar projects – see, e.g., Prasad et al. 2008). The human annotators themselves were asked to recognize discourse connectives in authentic texts. Therefore, a need for an accurate delimitation of discourse connectives arose, especially for stating the boundaries between connectives and non-connectives.

The most problematic issue appeared to be the multiword phrases like *to znamená* 'this means', *výsledkem bylo* 'the result was', *v důsledku toho* 'in consequence', *podmínkou je* 'the condition is' etc. These phrases clearly signal discourse relations within a text (e.g. *podmínkou je* 'the condition is' expresses a relation of condition), but they significantly differ (in lexico-syntactic as well as semantic aspect – see Rysová 2012) from the "prototypical", lexically frozen connectives like *ale* 'but' or *a* 'and' (these phrases may be inflected, appear in several variants[2] in the text etc. – see e.g. *za této podmínky* 'under this condition' vs. *za těchto podmínek* 'under these conditions', *závěrem je* 'the conclusion is' vs. *závěrem bylo* 'the conclusion was').

At the same time, some typical Czech connectives like *proto* 'therefore', *přesto* 'in spite of this' etc. were historically also multiword – they are frozen prepositional phrases (raised from the combination of preposition *pro* 'for' with the pronoun *to* 'this' and the preposition *přes* 'in spite of' with the pronoun *to* 'this'), so the main difference between them and present-day phrases like *kvůli tomu* 'due to this' is that they are now used as one-word expressions. This idea raises many questions – e.g. is the frozen lexical form (that appears in most of the typical present-day connectives in Czech) a sufficient argument to exclude the multiword phrases from discourse connectives and their annotation in the corpus? Would not the annotation without them be incomplete?

This led us to the idea to examine the historical origin of other 'prototypical' discourse connectives in Czech, which could tell us something about the men-

---

[1] To sentence information structure in Czech see, e.g., Hajičová, Partee & Sgall (2013) or Rysová (2014a).
[2] See also a study on reformulation markers by Cuenca (2003).

tioned multiword phrases in general and could suggest their uniform annotation in the corpus. In this respect, the paper concentrates on where to put the boundaries of discourse connectives so that the annotations of large corpus data are not incomplete and at the same time follow an adequate theoretical background.

4 Results and evaluation

4.1 Historical origin of the most frequent connectives in Czech

In these subsections, the paper presents the results of the analysis of discourse connectives with emphasis on their historical origin and development towards their present-day position in language. In this way, the paper introduces a comparative study of Czech, English and partly German.

Table 1: Most frequent Czech connectives in the PDiT

Czech connectives	Tokens in the PDiT
a 'and'	5,765
však 'however'	1,521
ale 'but'	1,267
když 'when'	574
protože 'because'	525
totiž 'that is'	460
pokud 'if'	403
proto 'therefore'	380
tedy 'so'	307
aby 'so that'	305

For the analysis, the ten most frequent discourse connectives in Czech (presented in Table 1) have been selected and their historical origin have been analyzed – see Table 2[3].

Table 2 demonstrates that none of the selected connectives was a connective from its origin. All of them arose from other parts of speech than conjunctions or structuring particles or from a combination of several words. At a certain

---

[2] The Czech connective *totiž* does not have an exact English counterpart; a similar meaning is carried by the German *nämlich*.

[3] The etymology of Czech connectives is adopted from the Czech etymological dictionaries and papers (see Holub & Kopečný (1952); Rejzek (2001); Bauer (1962); Bauer (1963)).

moment, this word or words began to be used in a connecting function, which started the process of their grammaticalization (cf. related works by Claridge & Arnovick 2010; Degand & Vandenbergen 2011; Claridge 2013 or Degand & Evers-Vermeul 2015).

This process began for the individual connectives in different periods (one of the oldest seems to be the rise of *a* 'and' in Czech as similarly *and* in English and *und* 'and' in German – see below). Sometimes the grammaticalization is not fully completed, which causes the discrepancies within some parts of speech (in Czech mainly within adverbs, particles and conjunctions). The unfinished grammaticalization is seen, e.g., on connectives that are still written as two words (like Czech *a tak* 'and so', *i když* 'even though' etc.) in contrast to already one-word connectives containing historically the same component *a* 'and' – *ale* 'but', *ač* 'although', *aby* 'so that'.

Table 2 shows that Czech present-day most frequent connectives originally arose from other parts of speech than, e.g., conjunctions, i.e. they are not connectives from their origin, but they gained a status of connectives during the historical development. Some of the Czech connectives arose from interjections (e.g. *a* 'and'), adverbs (e.g. *však* 'however') or adjectives (e.g. *také* 'too'). Most of them are originally compounds of two components (mainly interjections, particles, adverbs or prepositions). Some of the combinations even repeat – see combinations of preposition and pronoun (*pro-to* 'therefore', *při-tom* 'yet', *o-všem* 'nevertheless'), pronoun and particle (*te-dy* 'so', *co-ž* 'which') or preposition and adverb (*po-kud* 'if', *na-víc* 'moreover').

Some of the connectives are even combinations of three components – like preposition, pronoun and particle (*pro-to-že* 'because') or preposition and two pronouns (*za-tím-co* 'while'). Therefore, it is evident that the most frequent Czech connectives were (before they became one-word expressions) very similar to the present-day multiword phrases like *kvůli tomu* 'due to this' or *z tohoto důvodu* 'for this reason'. The origin of some of them is rather transparent even today (e.g. most native speakers are probably able to recognize that the connective *proto* 'therefore' is a compound of preposition *pro* 'for' and a pronoun *to* 'this') while some of them have (synchronically) lost motivation (see mainly the oldest connectives like *ale* 'but', *nebo* 'or' etc.). This fact is depending on the degree of their grammaticalization – the more grammaticalized the connective is, the less bonds remain to its historical origin. In this respect, discourse connectives are not a closed class of expressions, but rather a scale representing the process of connective grammaticalization.

2 The development of discourse connectives

Table 2: Historical origin of most frequent discourse connectives in Czech

Czech present-day connectives	Historical origin
a 'and'	from a deictic interjection meaning *hle* 'behold'
však 'however'	adverbial origin meaning 'always'
ale 'but'	combination of *a* 'and' (with interjectional origin) and particle *-le* (with the adverbial meaning *jen* 'only')
když 'when'	combination of adverb *kdy* 'when' and particle *-ž (že)* (today's conjunction 'that')
protože 'because'	combination of three components: preposition *pro* 'for', pronoun *to* 'this' and particle *-ž (že)* (today's conjunction 'that')
totiž 'that is'	unclear origin: either combination of three components: pronoun *to* 'this', particle *-ť (ti)* and particle *-ž (že)* (today's conjunction 'that') or grammaticalized verbal phrase *točúš/točíš* [lit. (you) it know] coming from the composition of a demonstrative pronoun *to* 'this' and a verb *čúti/číti*
pokud 'if'	combination of preposition *po* 'after' and adverb *kudy* 'from where'
proto 'therefore'	combination of preposition *pro* 'for' and pronoun *to* 'this'
tedy 'so'	combination of pronoun *to* 'this' and particle *-dy (-da)*
aby 'so that'	combination of *a* 'and' and verbal component *bych* (derived from the verb *být* 'be')

The given expressions in certain combinations and in certain forms begun to be used as connectives and they underwent the process of grammaticalization (in different time period) – thus, the individual present-day connectives lay in different parts of the scale according to the degree of their grammaticalization.

4.2 Historical origin of the most frequent connectives across languages

We have compared the results of analysis of Czech connectives with their counterparts in English[4] to see whether the connectives in another language exhibit similar behaviour – see Table 3.

Table 3[5] demonstrates that the origin of given English connectives is very comparable to their Czech counterparts. Also English connectives are not connectives from their origin. They arose also from other parts of speech (mainly from combinations of pronouns, prepositions and adverbs) or other multiword phrases. Many of them (not only presented in Table 3) have a pronominal origin (like *when, if, so, then, which*), many come from the whole phrases that may have two or more components – see the combination of an adverb and pronoun (*how-ever*) or adverb and preposition (*there-fore*).

Similar connective formation may be seen also in German.[6] For example, the connective *dass* 'so that, that' arose from a demonstrative pronoun *das* 'this', *jedoch* 'however' from the combination of two words: *je* 'sometimes' and conjunction *doch* 'however'.

The connective *nämlich* 'that is' (a counterpart to Czech *totiž*) is historically an unstressed variant of an adverb *name(nt)lich* 'namely' derived from the noun *Name* 'name'; the original meaning of *nämlich* is 'the same' but it shifted to present-day more often adverbial meaning of 'it means, more specifically'. The semantic shift is seen also in other German present-day connectives like *weil* 'because' (today, with a causal meaning, but originally expressing a temporal relation – cf. the German noun *Weile* 'moment' or English temporal conjunction *while*), *aber* 'but' (originally expressing multiple repetition like 'once again, again'), *wenn* 'when, if' (originally an unstressed variant of *wann* 'when' with

---

[4] Apart from the Czech connective *totiž* that does not have an appropriate counterpart in English (but it roughly corresponds to German connective *nämlich*).

[5] The etymology of English connectives is adopted from the English etymological dictionary – Harper (2001). The aim of this paper is not to discuss the etymology of English connectives in general (which is in detail in Lenker & Meurman-Solin (2007)), but to compare the origin of some of them with their Czech counterparts.

[6] The etymology of German connectives is adopted from Klein & Geyken (2010).

2 The development of discourse connectives

Table 3: Historical origin of selected discourse connectives in English

English present-day connectives	Historical origin
and	Old English *and, ond,* originally meaning 'thereupon, next' from Proto-Germanic *unda
however	combination of *how* and *ever* (late 14th century)
but	combination of West Germanic *be- 'by' and *utana 'out, outside, from without'; not used as conjunction in Old English
when	from pronominal stem *hwa-, from PIE interrogative base *kwo
because	combination of preposition *bi* and noun *cause: bi cause* 'by cause', often followed by a subordinate clause introduced by *that* or *why*; one word from around 1400
if	coming from Proto Indo-European pronominal stem *i-
therefore	combination of *there* and a preposition *fore* (an Old English and Middle English collateral form of the preposition *for*) meaning 'in consequence of that'
so	from Proto Indo-European reflexive pronominal stem *swo-, pronoun of the third person and reflexive
so that	unmerged conjunction of two components

temporal meaning; today, it expresses both temporal as well as conditional relations) etc.

A large group of present-day connectives arose from combination of prepositions and a deictic component *da* – see the so called anaphoric connectives like *dafür* lit. 'for this/that', *davor* 'previously', *danach* 'then', *darum* 'therefore' etc.

We see that the general principle of discourse connectives development was very similar in Czech, English as well as German. Therefore, it may be supposed that formation of discourse connectives is not language specific but language universal.

5 Formation of discourse connectives

5.1 General tendencies

In this part, the paper summarizes the most frequent formations for present-day discourse connectives (with more examples as well as from other languages) to demonstrate that there are some productive connective formations across the languages' development.

Firstly, the paper summarizes the general tendencies for connective formation in Czech. During the analysis above, we could observe that many of the Czech connectives follow similar principles and in some cases, they are formed even by the same components – see the following five points.

1. One of the most productive components (forming the final part of many Czech connectives) is the particle *-ž(e)*[7] occurring in the grammaticalized one-word connectives as well as in unmerged multiword phrases – see one-word examples like *což* 'which', *protože* 'because', *když* 'when', *též* 'too', *než* 'than', *nýbrž* 'but', *tudíž* 'thus', *až* 'until', *poněvadž* 'because', *jelikož* 'because', *jestliže* 'if'.

   This fact may help us in annotating the multiword phrases in large corpora like the Prague Discourse Treebank, specifically with the annotation of the extent of multiword phrases. In other words, we may better answer the questions like whether to annotate the whole phrases like *s podmínkou, že* 'with the condition that' or only *s podmínkou* 'with the condition' as a connective in examples like Example 1:

---

[7] Today's conjunction *že* 'that'.

2 The development of discourse connectives

(1) Rodiče mi dovolili koupit si psa **s podmínkou, že** úspěšně dodělám školu.

'My parents allowed me to buy a dog **with the condition that** I will successfully finish my school.'

Since we know that *-ž(e)* is a part of many one-word connectives in Czech (from a diachronic point of view), it is very likely also the part of yet non-grammaticalized phrases (that are, at the same time, replaceable by one-word connectives – e.g. the whole *s podmínkou, že* 'with the condition that' in Example 1 is replaceable by one-word *když* 'if', historically also containing the particle *-ž(e)*). In this respect, it may be expected that some of the similar multiword phrases will give rise to a new primary connective in the future, i.e. that *že* 'that' will become part of a new one-word connective as it happened in several cases in the past.

2. The conjunction (former interjection) *a* 'and' is a part of many present-day one-word connectives like *ale* 'but', *avšak* 'however', *ač* 'although', *anebo* 'or', *až* 'untill', *aby* 'so that' or unmerged *a tak* 'and so', *a proto* 'and therefore'. The tendency to combine with *a* 'and' is visible also in present-day multiword phrases (in intra-sentential usage) – see very often phrases like *a z tohoto důvodu* 'and for this reason', *a to znamená* 'and this means' etc.

3. Another productive formation of connectives is by the negative particle *ne* 'not' – see ***nebo*** 'or', ***neboť*** 'for', ***nýbrž***[8] 'but' or ***než*** 'than'.

4. Very frequent is also the combination with the former particle *-le* (with the meaning similar to 'only') – see connectives like *ale* 'but', *leč* 'however', *leda* 'unless' or *alespoň* 'at least'.

5. One of the most productive and also transparent means is the formation of discourse connectives in Czech by combination of prepositions (like *pro* 'for', *přes* 'over', *po* 'after', *za* 'behind', *před* 'before', *při* 'by', *na* 'on, at', *bez* 'without', *v* 'in', *nad* 'over' etc.) and pronouns (especially the demonstrative pronoun *to* 'this' in the whole paradigm) – see one-word examples like *proto* 'therefore', *přesto* 'yet, inspite of this', *potom* 'then', *zatím* 'meanwhile', *předtím* 'before', *přitom* 'yet, at the same time', *zato* 'however', *nato* 'then, after that', *beztoho* 'in any case', *vtom* 'suddenly', *nadto*

---

[8] Originally also *néberž(e), niebrž*.

'moreover'. Literally, *proto* means 'for this', *přesto* 'in spite of this', *potom* 'after this' etc.

Moreover, there are several present-day prepositional phrases (with discourse connective function) having exactly the same structure like the mentioned one-word connectives (i.e. they consist of a preposition and a demonstrative pronoun *to* 'this'; the only difference is that they have not merged into one-word expression) – see e.g. *kvůli tomu* 'because of this', *navzdory tomu* 'despite this', *kromě toho* 'besides this' etc. signaling discourse relations within a text. Therefore, we consider such prepositional phrases discourse connectives because they express discourse relations within a text and have a similar structure as some one-word connectives – the only difference is that their grammaticalization is not yet completed and that they are not merged into one-word expressions. So it seems that such formation of connectives from prepositional phrases is very productive (not only) in Czech.

A very similar process of discourse connective formation (i.e. from prepositional phrases) may be seen also in other languages, which supports its productivity across languages. The paper demonstrates this on the foreign counterparts of the Czech connective *proto* 'therefore' (that arose from the combination of the preposition *pro* 'for' and pronoun *to* 'this' as mentioned above). English *therefore* arose from the combination of *there* and *fore* (that was an Old English and Middle English collateral form of the preposition *for*) with the meaning 'in consequence of that'. Similar process may be seen in German *dafür* (from the preposition *für* 'for' and deictic component *da*) or parallelly Danish *derfor*. Moreover, there are many other English connectives with similar structure like *thereafter* (meaning 'after that'), *thereupon, therein, thereby, thereof, thereto* etc. or in German the productive anaphoric connectives like *davor* 'previously', *danach* 'then' etc. (see Section 4.2). All of these connectives follow the same formation principle (i.e. the anaphoric reference to the previous context plus the given preposition) that seems to be, therefore, language universal. There are similar unmerged phrases in English like *because of this, due to this* etc. as potential candidates for grammaticalization, i.e. as potential one-word fixed connectives.

We view the whole structures *because of this, due to this* as discourse connectives. As demonstrated above, there are some present-day primary connectives that historically arose from similar combination of a preposition and demonstrative pronoun (e.g. Czech connective *proto* 'therefore' etc.). At the same time, *because of, *due to themselves are ungrammatical structures (i.e. we cannot say *The weather is nice. *Due to, I will go to the beach.*) and need to combine with an anaphoric expression to gain a discourse connecting function. For these reasons, we consider the full structures to be the discourse connectives, i.e. including the demonstrative pronoun *this*.

5.2 Primary connectives and the process of grammaticalization

On the basis of previous analysis, the paper characterizes the most frequent (or prototypical) discourse connectives in the following way.

We use the term PRIMARY CONNECTIVES (firstly introduced by Rysová & Rysová 2014) for expressions with primary connective function (i.e. from part-of-speech membership, they are mainly conjunctions and structuring particles) that are mainly one-word and lexically frozen (from present-day perspective). Primary connectives are synsemantic (or functional) words so they are not integrated into clause structure as sentence elements. The primary connectives mostly do not allow modification (cf. **generally but*, **only and* etc., with some exceptions like *mainly because*). The most crucial aspect of primary connectives is that they underwent the process of grammaticalization, i.e. they arose from other parts of speech (cf., e.g., the connective *too* as the stressed variant of the preposition *to*) or combination of words (cf. English phrases *by cause* → *because, for the reason that* → *for, never the less* → *nevertheless* etc.), but they merged into a one-word expression during their historical development. Therefore, they underwent the gradual weakening or change of their original lexical meaning and fixing of the new form and function.

At the same time, primary connectives are not a strictly closed class of expressions. They are rather a scale mapping the process of their grammaticalization. This process is sometimes not fully completed so the primary connectives do not have to fulfill all the characteristics stated above – e.g. some of them are still written as two words (like Czech *i když* 'although' or English *as if, so that* etc.). The main argument here is that they fulfill most of the aspects and that their primary function in discourse is to connect two pieces of a text.

6 Multiword connecting phrases

6.1 Secondary connectives: Potential candidates for primary connectives?

Apart from primary connectives, also another specific group among discourse connectives may be distinguished – the SECONDARY CONNECTIVES (the term firstly used by Rysová & Rysová 2014). The reason is (as discussed above) that primary connectives are not the only expressions with the ability to signal discourse relations. There are also multiword phrases like *this is the reason why, generally speaking, the result is, it was caused by, this means that* etc. These phrases also express discourse relations within a text (e.g. *generally speaking* signals a relation of generalization), but they significantly differ from primary connectives – mostly, they may be inflected (*for this reason – for these reasons*), modified (*the main/important/only condition is*) and they exhibit a high degree of variation in authentic texts (the variation is better seen in inflected Czech – see, e.g., secondary connectives *příkladem je* vs. *příklad je* both meaning 'the example is', firstly used in instrumental, secondly in nominative). Therefore, secondary connectives may be defined as an open class of expressions.

Generally, secondary connectives are multiword phrases (forming open or fixed collocations) containing an autosemantic (i.e. lexical) component or components. Secondary connectives function as sentence elements (e.g. *due to this*), clause modifiers (*simply speaking*) or even as separate sentences (*the result was clear*). Concerning part-of-speech membership, secondary connectives are a very heterogeneous group of expressions – very often, they contain nouns like *difference, reason, condition, cause, exception, result, consequence, conclusion* etc. (i.e. nouns that directly indicate the semantic type of discourse relations), similarly verbs like *to mean, to contrast, to explain, to cause, to justify, to precede, to follow* etc. and prepositions like *due to, because of, in spite of, in addition to, unlike, on the basis of* (functioning as secondary connectives only in combination with an anaphoric reference to the previous unit of text realized mostly by the pronoun *this* – cf. *due to this, because of this* etc.).[9]

All of these aspects indicate that secondary connectives have not yet undergone the process of grammaticalization although they exhibit some of its features – e.g. gradual stabilization or preference of one form or gradual weakening of the original lexical meaning (see Section 6.3).

Within the secondary connectives, the most frequent structures occurring in the PDiT have also been analyzed – see Table 4 (the analysis was done on the annotation of secondary connectives in the PDiT – see Rysová & Rysová 2014; 2015). Table 4 presents the tokens for the individual forms of the secondary connectives, i.e. not lemmas. The aim was to see which concrete form of the same secondary connective is the most frequent and has the biggest chance to become fixed or stable in the future. For example, the PDiT contains the secondary connective *to znamená, že* 'this means that', but also the similar variants like *znamená to, že* [lit.

---

[9] This type of secondary connectives may be detected in the corpus automatically – see Rysová & Mírovský (2014).

means this that] 'this means that'. In this case, the most frequent is the variant *to znamená, že* 'this means that' with 22 tokens in the PDiT (see Table 4). A high degree of variability is also one of the reasons why secondary connectives are very difficult to annotate in large corpora.

We see that the frequency of the individual secondary connectives is much lower than of the primary connectives (presented in Table 1). The most frequent secondary connective in the PDiT is the verbal phrase *dodal* '(he) added'[10] with 121 tokens. Very frequent secondary connectives are also represented by prepositional phrases (like *v případě, že* 'in case that', *v této souvislosti* 'in this regard'), often in the combination with the demonstrative pronoun *to* 'this' (like *kromě toho* 'besides this' or *naproti tomu* 'in contrast to this'), which is historically a very productive formation of primary connectives (see Section 5.1). One of the most frequent secondary connectives in Czech (in the PDiT) is also the prepositional phrase *z tohoto důvodu* 'for this reason' that is very similar to the Old English phrases such as *for þon þy* literally 'for the (reason) that' giving probably the rise of the present-day English connective *for*.

So it may be observed that the present-day secondary connectives have very similar structures as the former ones and that the process of connective formation thus repeats across the historical development. In very simple terms, the secondary connectives often become primary through the long process of grammaticalization; simultaneously, some new secondary connectives are rising, as well as some old primary connectives are disappearing – cf., e.g., the Old Czech expressions *an, ana, ano* (lit. 'and he', 'and she', 'and it') being used as connectives for different semantic relations (e.g. conjunction, opposition or reason and result). These expressions were used still in the first half of the 19th century but then they gradually lost their position in language and completely disappeared (see Grepl 1956). In this respect, discourse connectives represent a dynamic complex or set of expressions with stable centre (containing grammaticalized primary connectives) and variable periphery (containing non-grammaticalized secondary connectives).

6.2 Other connecting phrases

During the analysis of the PDiT data, it have been observed that there are also big differences among the multiword connecting phrases themselves – cf. the phrases like *navzdory tomu* 'despite this', *navzdory tomuto faktu* 'despite this fact', *navzdory této situaci* 'despite this situation', *navzdory této myšlence* 'despite

---

[10] For more details to verbs of saying functioning as secondary connectives see Rysová (2014b).

Table 4: Most frequent secondary connectives in the PDiT

Secondary connectives	Tokens in the PDiT
dodal '(he) added'	121
podobně 'similarly'	60
v případě, že 'in case that'	40
vzhledem k tomu, že 'concerning the fact that'	40
dodává '(he) adds'	36
kromě toho 'besides this'	30
naproti tomu 'in contrast to this'	23
to znamená, že 'this means that'	22
v této souvislosti 'in this regard'	17
případně 'possibly'	13
příkladem je 'the example is'	12
upřesnil '(he) specified'	12
znamená to, že [lit. means this that] 'this means that'	12
z tohoto důvodu 'for this reason'	11

this idea', etc. (all occurring in the authentic Czech texts). All of these phrases clearly signal a discourse relation of concession, but they do not have the same function in structuring of discourse. The difference is that the phrases like *navzdory tomu* 'despite this' may function as discourse connectives in many various contexts (with the relation of concession), i.e. their status of discourse connectives is almost universal or context independent. On the other hand, phrases like *navzdory této myšlence* 'despite this idea' fit only into certain contexts, i.e. they function as indicators of discourse relations only occasionally, not universally (although they contribute to the whole compositional structure of text and participate in text coherence) – see Examples 2 and 3:

(2) Vše začalo nemilým ranním probuzením, všude byla mlha. **Navzdory tomu** jsem sedl do vlaku a odjel.

'Everything started with unpleasant morning awakening, the fog was everywhere. **Despite this**, I sat on the train and left.'

(3) Uvažovali jsme o modernizaci školy a knihovny. **Navzdory této myšlence** došlo z finančních důvodů pouze k rozvoji knihovny.

'We considered modernization of our school and library. **Despite this idea**, we have developed only the library for financial reasons.'

2 The development of discourse connectives

The expression *navzdory tomu* 'despite this' in Example 2 expresses a discourse relation of concession and may be used also in Example 3 (cf. ***Despite this***, *we have developed only the library for financial reasons.*). On the other hand, the expression *navzdory této myšlence* 'despite this idea' is more context dependent, i.e. it signals a discourse relation of concession in Example 3 but it cannot be used in Example 2 (cf. *Everything started with unpleasant morning awakening, the fog was everywhere.* ****Despite this idea**, I sat on the train and left.*).

This universality (or context independency) is considered a crucial feature of discourse connectives (both primary and secondary) and the boundary between connectives and non-connectives may be put right here, i.e. according to the universality principle.[11] Discourse connectives are thus expressions with (almost) universal connective function, i.e. the author may choose them for signaling given semantic type of discourse relations almost in any context.[12] We do not consider the other phrases (also signaling discourse relations, but only in certain contexts) to be discourse connectives and we call them (non-universal) free connecting phrases.

This paper has tried to demonstrate the heterogeneity of connective means in general (going from grammaticalized primary connectives to variable secondary connectives and free connecting phrases).

6.3 Annotations of discourse connectives and other connecting phrases in large corpora

We believe that the detailed linguistic analysis of discourse connectives and other phrases may help in processing these expressions in large corpora like the Prague Discourse Treebank. As demonstrated above, there are many possibilities to express discourse relations in a language – by one-word, monomorphematic expressions as well as variable multiword phrases. So the annotation in the corpora should react to their variability and different linguistic nature.

At the same time, the annotation of discourse connectives and other connecting phrases in large corpora may significantly help their further examination in terms of how these expressions usually behave in authentic texts.

---

[11] Universality principle evaluates linguistic expressions from very lexical point of view (i.e. their degree of concreteness and abstractness). It does not reflect, e.g., the differences in register, the degree of subjectivity (cf. the differences between *since* and *because* in English) etc., see Rysová & Rysová 2015.
[12] We are aware that expressions like *and, but, on the other hand* etc. have also other (non-connective) meanings (cf. *girls and boys*). However, these other meanings are not in our interest – we evaluate the expressions only in their connective function.

The Prague Discourse Treebank contains the annotation of primary connectives (finished in 2012 as PDiT 1.0, see Poláková et al. 2012) and newly also of secondary connectives and other free connecting phrases (published in 2016 as PDiT 2.0, see Rysová et al. 2016); for more information see Rysová & Rysová 2014).[13] Altogether, primary connectives represent 94.6% (20,255 tokens) and secondary connectives 5.4% (1,161 tokens) within all discourse connectives in the PDiT (i.e. altogether 21,416 tokens). So the terms primary and secondary connectives correspond also to their frequency in large corpora. In addition to discourse connectives, the PDiT contains also the annotation of the free connecting phrases (like *despite this idea* etc.) with altogether 151 tokens.

In the current stage, the PDiT thus contains the annotation of explicit discourse relations based on a deep linguistic research, i.e. reflecting all the differences among the individual connective expressions.

The results of the annotation in the PDiT demonstrate that the authors of authentic texts mostly use the grammaticalized primary connectives, then non-grammaticalized secondary connectives and lastly the contextually dependent free connecting phrases. The reasons may be that primary connectives are lexically frozen, short, very often one-word expressions that are not (as functional words) integrated into clause structure. Their usage in texts may thus be related to economy in language, i.e. the author chooses the easiest (or the most economical) solution.

6.4 Secondary connectives in the PDiT vs. alternative lexicalizations of discourse connectives in the PDTB

In the last section, this paper shortly compares the above mentioned approach to discourse connectives in the Prague Discourse Treebank (PDiT) with discourse connectives in the Penn Discourse Treebank (PDTB, see Prasad, Webber & Joshi 2014). The PDTB is one of the richest corpora with discourse annotation and it inspired also the annotation of connectives in the PDiT. Therefore, the paper introduces here where the PDTB and PDiT annotations meet as well as differ with emphasis on multiword discourse phrases (called secondary connectives in the PDiT and alternative lexicalizations of discourse connectives, i.e. AltLexes, in the PDTB).

---

[13] The inter-annotator agreement on the existence of discourse relations expressed by secondary connectives reached 0.70 F1, agreement of semantic types of relations expressed by secondary connectives is 0.82 (i.e. 0.78 Cohen's κ, see Rysová & Rysová 2015).

2 The development of discourse connectives

The difference in terminology is given by the different approach to discourse connectives in both projects. The terminology reflects especially the annotation strategies of the PDiT and the PDTB that may be briefly described in the following points.

PDTB:

- EXPLICIT CONNECTIVES (18,459 annotated tokens) – established according to a list of connectives collected from various sources (cf. e.g. Halliday & Hasan 1976; Martin 1992) and updated during the annotations of authentic Wall Street Journal texts; explicit connectives are here restricted to the following syntactic classes: subordinating and coordinating conjunctions, prepositional phrases, adverbs; examples: *so, when, and, while, in comparison, on the other hand, as a result* (see Prasad, Joshi & Webber 2010);

- ALTLEXES (624 annotated tokens) – discovered during the annotation of implicit relations; the emphasis is placed on the redundancy of AltLexes and explicit connectives in signaling one discourse relation in the same sentence; there are no grammatical restrictions on AltLexes except for they do not belong to explicit connectives – AltLexes are thus viewed as alternatives to explicit connectives; annotation was carried out only between two adjacent sentences; examples: *for one thing, one reason is, never mind that, adding to that speculation, the increase was due mainly to, a consequence of their departure could be* (see Prasad, Joshi & Webber 2010).

PDiT:

- PRIMARY CONNECTIVES (20,255 annotated tokens) – the emphasis is placed on the origin and general characteristics of connectives; primary connectives are mostly grammaticalized synsemantics (grammatical words) without the function of sentence elements; lexically, they are context independent, i.e. they function as primary connectives in many contexts; the annotators were not provided by the list of connectives but acquainted with the general definition; examples: *so, when, and, while*;

- SECONDARY CONNECTIVES (1,161 annotated tokens) – they are non-grammaticalized expressions or phrases with the function of sentence elements or sentence modifiers containing lexical (autosemantic) element; lexically, they are context independent, i.e. they function as secondary connectives in many contexts; they are annotated as a separate group on the whole PDiT data; examples: *in comparison, on the other hand, as a result, for one thing, one reason is, never mind that*;

- OTHER CONNECTIVE MEANS: FREE CONNECTING PHRASES (151 annotated tokens) – they are mainly multiword phrases with a high degree of concreteness or lexicality that are highly dependent on context; their annotation is carried out on the whole PDiT data; examples: *adding to that speculation, the increase was due mainly to, a consequence of their departure could be.*

As we see, both projects look at discourse connectives from slightly different perspective or different point of view, which is reflected both in terminology as well as annotation principles.

7 Conclusion

The paper introduced the analysis of historical formation of discourse connectives especially in Czech. It supports the idea that present-day lexically frozen connectives (called primary) arose from other parts of speech (especially from particles, adverbs and prepositions) or combinations of two or more words. In other words, primary connectives were not primary connectives from their origin but they gained this status during their historical development – through the process of grammaticalization. In this respect, we do not define discourse connectives as a closed class of expressions but rather a scale mapping the grammaticalization of the individual connective expressions.

At the same time, there are two specific groups of discourse connectives: primary and secondary. They differ mainly in the fact in which place on the scale they occur, i.e. whether the process of grammaticalization is already completed (or is in its final phase) or whether this process has just started. In this respect, primary connectives are mainly one-word, lexically frozen, grammatical expressions with primary connecting function and secondary connectives are mainly multiword structures containing lexical (autosemantic) word or words, functioning as sentence elements, clause modifiers or even separate sentences. Both primary and secondary connectives are defined on the basis of their context independency (i.e. on their suitability to function as connectives for given semantic relation in many various contexts).

Since the present-day primary connectives arose from similar phrases or parts of speech like secondary connectives (and very often from combination of several words that gradually merged together – with some possible losses), we look at the secondary connectives as at the potential primary connectives in the future.

The paper has also analyzed another group of connective expressions – the free connecting phrases (like *despite this idea, because of these activities* etc.) functioning as discourse indicators only occasionally, depending on certain contexts, i.e. these phrases do not have a universal status of discourse connectives (as both primary and secondary) and they exhibit a high degree of variation.

The paper has shown the etymology and historical origin of the most frequent discourse connectives especially in Czech, English and German. It was found out that the examined connectives exhibit a similar behaviour and that they underwent a similar process of formation. In this respect, tha paper suggests that the rise and ways of formation of discourse connectives is (to large extent) language universal.

The analysis may help with the annotation of discourse in large corpora, as the annotation principles should react to the differences among the individual connective expressions and should be based on a detailed theoretical research. We have carried out such annotation in the Prague Discourse Treebank (on almost 50 thousand sentences) to observe how these expressions behave in authentic texts and what is their frequency in the large corpus data. We found out that primary connectives represent 94.6% and secondary connectives 5.4% within all discourse connectives in the PDiT. The most frequent secondary connectives have very similar structures that gave rise to present-day primary connectives.

Acknowledgments

The author acknowledges support from the Czech Science Foundation (Grant Agency of the Czech Republic): project GA CR No. 17-06123S (Anaphoricity in Connectives: Lexical Description and Bilingual Corpus Analysis). This work has been using language resources developed, stored and distributed by the LINDAT/CLARIN project of the Ministry of Education, Youth and Sports of the Czech Republic (project LM2015071).

The author gratefully thanks Jiří Mírovský from the Charles University for providing quantitative data on the basis of the PDiT for this paper.

References

Aijmer, Karin. 2002. *English discourse particles: Evidence from a corpus.* Vol. 10. Amsterdam: John Benjamins Publishing.

Bauer, Jaroslav. 1962. Spojky a příslovce [Conjunctions and adverbs]. *Sborník prací FF BU, A10* 11. 29–37.

Bauer, Jaroslav. 1963. Podíl citoslovcí na vzniku českých spojek [The importance of interjections in the development of Czech conjunctions]. *Sborník prací FF BU, A* 11. 21–28.

Claridge, Claudia. 2013. The evolution of three pragmatic markers: As it were, so to speak/say and if you like. *Journal of Historical Pragmatics* 14(2). 161–184.

Claridge, Claudia & Leslie Arnovick. 2010. Pragmaticalisation and discursisation. *Historical Pragmatics* 8. 165–169.

Cuenca, Maria-Josep. 2003. Two ways to reformulate: A contrastive analysis of reformulation markers. *Journal of Pragmatics* 35(7). 1069–1093.

Degand, Liesbeth & Jacqueline Evers-Vermeul. 2015. Grammaticalization or pragmaticalization of discourse markers?: More than a terminological issue. *Journal of Historical Pragmatics* 16(1). 59–85.

Degand, Liesbeth & Anne-Marie Simon Vandenbergen. 2011. Introduction: Grammaticalization and (inter) subjectification of discourse markers. *Linguistics* 49(2). 287–294.

Fischer, Kerstin. 2006. *Approaches to discourse particles.* Amsterdam: Elsevier.

Fraser, Bruce. 1999. What are discourse markers? *Journal of Pragmatics* 31(7). 931–952.

Grepl, Miroslav. 1956. Spojka an... Ve spisovném jazyce první poloviny 19. Století. *Sborník prací Filosofické fakulty brněnské university A* 4 5. 45–50.

Hajičová, Eva, Barbara Partee & Petr Sgall. 2013. *Topic-focus articulation, tripartite structures, and semantic content.* Springer Science & Business Media.

Hakulinen, Auli. 1998. The use of Finnish nyt as a discourse particle. *Pragmatics and Beyond New Series* 57. 83–96.

Halliday, Michael A. K. & Ruqaiya Hasan. 1976. *Cohesion in English.* London: Longman.

Hansen, Maj-Britt Mosegaard. 1998. *The function of discourse particles: A study with special reference to spoken standard French.* Vol. 53. Amsterdam: John Benjamins Publishing.

Harper, Douglas et al. 2001. *Online etymology dictionary.* http://etymonline.com/.

Holub, Josef & František Kopečný. 1952. *Etymologický slovník jazyka českého* [Etymological dictionary of Czech]. Prague: Státní nakladatelství učebnic v Praze.

Klein, Wolfgang & Alexander Geyken. 2010. Das Digitale Wörterbuch der Deutschen Sprache (DWDS). *Lexicographica* 26. 79–93.

Lenker, Ursula & Anneli Meurman-Solin. 2007. *Connectives in the history of English*. Amsterdam: John Benjamins Publishing.

Martin, James R. 1992. *English text: System and structure*. Amsterdam: John Benjamins Publishing.

Maschler, Yael. 2000. *Discourse markers in bilingual conversation*. Kingston Press Services.

Poláková, Lucie, Pavlína Jínová, Šárka Zikánová, Eva Hajičová, Jiří Mírovský, Anna Nedoluzhko, Magdaléna Rysová, Veronika Pavlíková, Jana Zdeňková, Jiří Pergler & Radek Ocelák. 2012. *Prague Discourse Treebank 1.0*. Prague, Czech Republic: ÚFAL MFF UK.

Prasad, Rashmi, Aravind K. Joshi & Bonnie Webber. 2010. Realization of discourse relations by other means: Alternative lexicalizations. In *Proceedings of the 23rd International Conference on Computational Linguistics: Posters*, 1023–1031. Association for Computational Linguistics.

Prasad, Rashmi, Bonnie Webber & Aravind K. Joshi. 2014. Reflections on the Penn Discourse Treebank, comparable corpora, and complementary annotation. *Computational Linguistics* 40(4). 921–950.

Prasad, Rashmi, Nikhil Dinesh, Alan Lee, Eleni Miltsakaki, Livio Robaldo, Aravind K. Joshi & Bonnie L. Webber. 2008. The Penn Discourse TreeBank 2.0. In *Proceedings of LREC 2008*.

Rejzek, Jiří. 2001. *Český etymologický slovník [Czech etymological dictionary]*. nakladatelství LEDA.

Rysová, Kateřina. 2014a. *O slovosledu z komunikačního pohledu [On word order from the communicative point of view]* (Studies in Computational and Theoretical Linguistics). Prague: ÚFAL.

Rysová, Magdaléna, Pavlína Synková, Jiří Mírovský, Eva Hajičová, Anna Nedoluzhko, Radek Ocelák, Jiří Pergler, Lucie Poláková, Veronika Pavlíková, Jana Zdeňková & Šárka Zikánová. 2016. *Prague Discourse Treebank 2.0*. Prague, Czech Republic: ÚFAL MFF UK.

Rysová, Magdaléna. 2012. Alternative lexicalizations of discourse connectives in Czech. In *Proceedings of the 8th International Conference on Language Resources and Evaluation (LREC 2012)*, 2800–2807. Istanbul, Turkey: European Language Resources Association.

Rysová, Magdaléna. 2014b. Verbs of saying with a textual connecting function in the Prague Discourse Treebank. In *Proceedings of the Ninth International Con-*

ference on Language Resources and Evaluation (LREC 2014), 930–935. Reykjavik, Island: European Language Resources Association.

Rysová, Magdaléna & Jiří Mírovský. 2014. Use of coreference in automatic searching for multiword discourse markers in the Prague Dependency Treebank. In Lori Levin & Manfred Stede (eds.), *Proceedings of The 8th Linguistic Annotation Workshop (LAW-VIII)*, 11–19. Dublin City University (DCU). Dublin, Ireland: Dublin City University (DCU).

Rysová, Magdaléna & Kateřina Rysová. 2014. The centre and periphery of discourse connectives. In Wirote Aroonmanakun, Prachya Boonkwan & Thepchai Supnithi (eds.), *Proceedings of the 28th Pacific Asia Conference on Language, Information and Computing*, 452–459. Department of Linguistics, Faculty of Arts, Chulalongkorn University. Bangkok, Thailand: Department of Linguistics, Faculty of Arts, Chulalongkorn University.

Rysová, Magdaléna & Kateřina Rysová. 2015. Secondary connectives in the Prague Dependency Treebank. In Eva Hajičová & Joakim Nivre (eds.), *Proceedings of the Third International Conference on Dependency Linguistics (Depling 2015)*, 291–299. Uppsala, Sweden: Uppsala University.

Schiffrin, Deborah. 1987. *Discourse markers*. Cambridge: Cambridge University Press.

Schourup, Lawrence. 1999. Discourse markers. *Lingua* 107(3). 227–265.

Shloush, Shelley. 1998. A unified account of Hebrew bekicur 'in short': Relevance theory and discourse structure considerations. *Discourse Markers: Descriptions and Theory* 57. 61–82.

Urgelles-Coll, Miriam. 2010. *The syntax and semantics of discourse markers*. London: Continuum International.

Zwicky, Arnold M. 1985. Clitics and particles. *Language* 61(2). 283–305.

Chapter 3

Possibilities of text coherence analysis in the Prague Dependency Treebank

Kateřina Rysová

Charles University, Faculty of Mathematics and Physics

> The aim of this paper is to examine the interplay of text coreference and sentence information structure and its role in text coherence. The study is based on the analysis of authentic Czech texts from the Prague Dependency Treebank 3.0 (PDT; i.e. on almost 50 thousand sentences). The corpus contains manual annotation of both text coreference and information structure – the paper tries to demonstrate how these two different corpus annotations may be used in examination of text coherence. In other words, the paper tries to describe where these two language phenomena meet and how important the interplay is in making text well comprehensible for the reader. Our results may be used not only in a theoretical way but also practically in automatic corpus annotations, as they may give us an answer to the general question whether it is possible to annotate the sentence information structure automatically in large corpora on the basis of text coreference.

1 Introduction and theoretical background

Studying text coherence is dependent on studying several individual language phenomena like coreference, anaphora, sentence information structure or discourse (mainly in terms of semantico-pragmatic discourse relations). In other words, a text may be imagined as a net of many different kinds of relations that are mutually interconnected and possibly influence each other.

So far, these phenomena have been studied primarily in isolation but recently, there is a growing need for more complex studies focusing on interaction (see, for example, Hajičová, Hladká & Kučová 2006; Hajičová 2011; Eckert & Strube 2000;

Kateřina Rysová. 2017. Possibilities of text coherence analysis in the Prague Dependency Treebank. In Katrin Menzel, Ekaterina Lapshinova-Koltunski & Kerstin Kunz (eds.), *New perspectives on cohesion and coherence*, 33–45. Berlin: Language Science Press. DOI:10.5281/zenodo.814462

Rysová & Rysová 2015). In other words, if we want to analyze text coherence deeply (i.e. to help to answer the question what are the general properties of a text), we have to pay closer attention to the interactions of several individual phenomena at once (operating both inter- and intra-sententially).[1]

The theme of interplay between coreference or anaphoric relations and sentence information structure has been studied recently especially in Nedoluzhko & Hajičová (2015) and Nedoluzhko (2015) who linguistically investigated contextually bound nominal expressions (explicitly present in the sentence) that do not have an anaphoric (bridging, coreference or segment) link to a previous (con)text. They draw the conclusion that three cases may be found when contextually bound expressions may not be linked by any coreference or anaphoric relation: (i) contextually bound nominal groups related to previous context (semantically or pragmatically) but not specified as bridging relations in the Prague Dependency Treebank (PDT); (ii) noun groups referring to secondary circumstances (like temporal, local, etc.) and (iii) nominal groups having low referential potential.

In this respect, this paper follows their work. It investigates a narrower data sample (only expressions interlinked by text coreference) with the aim to bring an overview of density of text coreference relations according to the sentence information structure values of the interlinked expressions.

The complex analysis of text coherence demands extensive language material of authentic texts, i.e. large language corpora with multilayer annotation. Such corpora are rather rare (cf., for example, Komen 2012; Stede & Neumann 2014; Chiarcos 2014). The corpus with one of the richest (i.e. multilayer) annotation is the Prague Dependency Treebank (PDT) for Czech (see Bejček et al. 2013). The PDT contains detailed annotation on morphological, analytical (surface syntactic) and tectogrammatical (deep syntactic) level as well as the annotation of sentence information structure, coreference and anaphoric relations, discourse relations and text genres. The PDT thus offers suitable language material for studies focusing on the annotated language phenomena in interaction.

The paper concentrates on the interplay of two of them – text coreference and sentence information structure (mainly in terms of contextual boundness) – as well as on the fact how and to what extent this interplay is projected into text coherence.

---

[1] For complex studying of coherence phenomena, see Accessibility Theory (Ariel 1988) or Centering Theory (Joshi & Weinstein 1981; Grosz & Sidner 1986).

2 Main objectives

Generally, as said above, the paper focuses on the relation between text coreference and sentence information structure. It describes where and in which aspects these two phenomena meet in the text and how they influence each other. It also presents methods that may be used for analyzing language interplays in general (demonstrated using the PDT data). Finally, the paper demonstrates whether and how the present (manual) annotation of text coreference in the PDT may be used for improving automatic annotation of sentence information structure.

To meet the goals, the paper focuses on the specific tasks concerning the relation of text coreference and sentence information structure (in sense of contextual boundness – see §3.1). The paper explores whether the text coreference relations (in the PDT texts) connect rather contextually bound or non-bound sentence members (mutually) or both of them in the same way, see Examples 1 and 2 and Figure 1 below.

Since the contextually bound sentence items usually carry information that is deducible from the previous (con)text (in contrast to the contextually non-bound items), we assume the higher number of text coreference links leading right from them. In other words, the assumption is that text coreference and sentence information structure meet especially in sentence items related somehow to the previous (con)text.

3 Methods and material

3.1 Sentence information structure in the PDT

The analysis uses the language data of the Prague Dependency Treebank. The PDT contains almost 50,000 sentences (833,195 word tokens in 3,165 documents) of Czech newspaper texts that are (mostly manually) annotated on several language levels at once.

The theoretical framework for sentence information structure in the PDT is based on Functional Generative Description (FGD) introduced by Sgall (1967) and further developed especially by Hajičová, Partee & Sgall (1998).

The annotation is carried out on tectogrammatical trees. Each relevant node of the tree is labeled with one of the three values of contextual boundness.[2] Contextual boundness has the following possible values: non-contrastive contextually

---

[2] In addition, the communicative dynamism is annotated – as deep order of the nodes in the tree.

bound nodes (marked as "t"), contrastive contextually bound nodes (marked as "c") and contextually non-bound nodes (marked as "f").

Non-contrastive contextually bound nodes represent units that are considered deducible from the broad (not necessarily verbatim) context and are known for the reader (or presented as known for him or her). Contrastive contextually bound nodes also are expressions related to the broad context and moreover, they usually represent a choice from a set of alternatives. They often occur at the beginning of paragraphs, in enumerations etc. In spoken language, such units carry an optional contrastive stress. Contextually non-bound expressions are not presented as known and are not deducible from the previous context – on the contrary, they represent new facts (or known facts in new relations). The particular occurrences of contextual boundness values can be found in (1).

(1) [*Jane is my friend.*] She.t is.f very.f fine.f. However, her.t brother.c is.t boring.f. I.t like.f rather.f her.f.

On the basis of contextual boundness, the division of the sentence into Topic and Focus is realized (Topic is formed especially by contextually bound items and Focus typically by non-bound items). In the first sentence, the Topic is *she* and the Focus *is very fine*. In the second sentence, the Topic part includes *however, her brother is* and the Focus part *boring*. The participant *I* is the Topic of the third sentence and the part *like rather her* is the Focus.[3]

For further examples of "t", "c" and "f" nodes, see (2) in §3.3. For more details about Topic-Focus Articulation, see Hajičová, Partee & Sgall (1998).

3.2 Text coreference in the PDT

Annotation principles of text coreference in the PDT were done according to Nedoluzhko (2011). In this concept, the text coreference is understood as the use of different language means for marking the same object of textual reference. The basic principle of text coreference is that the antecedent and the anaphor referents are identical (e.g. *a house – the house; Jane – she – her; Jane – 0; problem – this – that*).

The general aspect of text coreference is that the coreferential relation is symmetric (if A is coreferential with B, B is coreferential with A) and transitive (if A is coreferential with B and B is coreferential with C, then A is coreferential with C).

---

[3] For more details about annotation of sentence information structure in English texts, see Rysová, Rysová & Hajičová (2015).

3 Text coherence in the PDT

Text coreference relations in the PDT are represented especially by personal or possessive pronouns (*Jane – she – her*), ellipsis (*Jane – 0*), demonstratives (*problem – this – that*) or by referential nominal phrases (concerning mainly nouns with specific, abstract or generic reference – for more details see Nedoluzhko (2011)) and they operate both inter- and intra-sententially.

3.3 Example of a dependency tree from the Prague Dependency Treebank

(2) illustrates the most common corpus occurrence – the text coreference connection leading from a non-contrastive contextually bound node to another non-contrastive contextually bound node (i.e. from "t" to "t").

(2) [Jestliže ve státě New Hampshire začne geometricky narůstat kriminalita mladistvých, veřejnost ocení svou přízní vládní akt zvýšení výdajů na boj se zločinností.]] Takové dobré **opatření** nakonec udělá každá druhá vláda, zvlášť půjde-li o **opatření** předvolební.

[If the juvenile delinquency will increase in the state of New Hampshire, the public will appreciate the government act to increase spending on the fight against crime.] Every other government eventually makes such good **measure**, regarding especially a pre-election **measure**.

Figure 1 represents the sentence from (2). The text coreference arrow leads from the second occurrence of the word *measure* (non-contrastive contextually bound ("t")) to the first occurrence of the word *measure* (that is also non-contrastive contextually bound ("t"), i.e. deducible from the previous context).

Another coreference relation is between the nodes *government* (Figure 1) and *government* (*act*) from the previous sentence, see (2). In Figure 1, only the starting position of this coreference relation can be seen. The final position of the coreference arrow is in the previous tree in the treebank and it is not displayed in Figure 1.

3.4 PML Tree Query

Our analysis of the interaction between information structure and text coreference was carried out with the client-server PML Tree Query (PML-TQ; the primary format of the PDT is called Prague Markup Language) (Štěpánek & Pajas 2010). The client part has been implemented as an extension to the tree editor TrEd (Pajas & Štěpánek 2008) that may be used also for editing data.

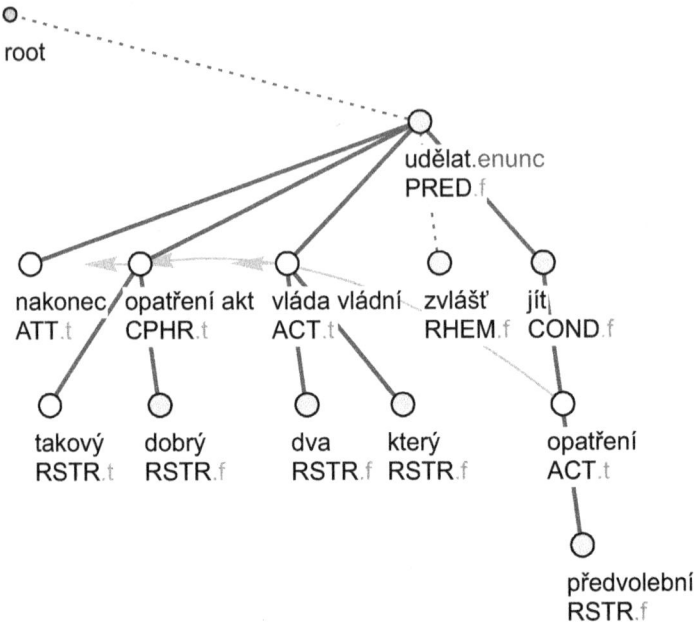

Figure 1: Dependency tree from the Prague Dependency Treebank depicting the sentence *Takové dobré opatření nakonec udělá každá druhá vláda, zvlášť půjde-li o opatření předvolební.* – Every other government eventually makes such good measure, regarding especially a pre-election measure.

Using PML-TQ engine, all the occurrences of text coreference relations in the PDT (annotated as arrows – see Figure 1) have been collected and we have examined the information structure of the sentence items (nodes in dependency trees) where the text coreference relations start and where they lead to. In other words, identifying whether the items participating in text coreference are rather contextually bound or non-bound.

4 Results and evaluation

Table 1 shows text coreference relations connecting contextually bound and non-bound sentence items (nodes) in the PDT.[4]

From the comparison of Figure 2 and 3, we may observe that among all the 86,590 text coreference relations marked in the PDT, mainly the non-contrastive

---

[4] The distributions of "f", "t" and "c" nodes in the PDT are presented below.

Table 1: Contextually bound and non-bound sentence items interconnected with text coreference relation in the Prague Dependency Treebank

	f (from)	t (from)	c (from)	To (in total)
f (to)	19,571	20,354	2,754	42,679
t (to)	7,980	27,109	1,762	36,851
c (to)	2,322	3,671	1,067	7,060
>From (in total)	29,873	51,134	5,583	**86,590**

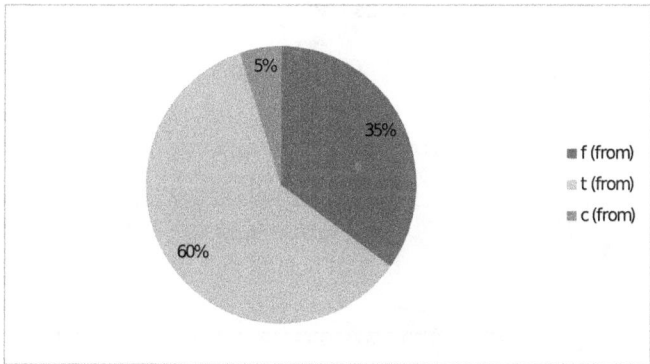

Figure 2: Percentage of individual node types participating in text coreference as the sender of the coreference arrow (its starting point)

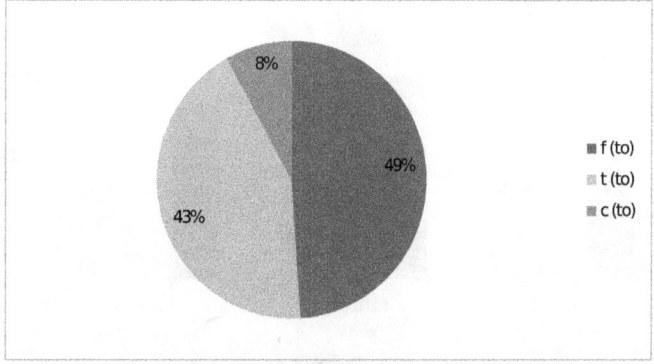

Figure 3: Percentage of individual node types participating in text coreference as the recipient of the coreference arrow (its ending point)

contextually bound sentence items ("t" nodes) (60%) are referring to the previous text (51,134 within 86,590). On the contrary, mainly the contextually non-bound sentence items ("f" nodes) (49%) serve as recipients of text coreference relations (42,679 within 86,590), see Figure 2. More specifically, if there is the coreference text relation between the words *Jane* and *she* (i.e. from *she* to *Jane*), *she* is mostly (in 60%) "t" node (i.e. non-contrastive contextually bound sentence item) and *Jane*, on the other hand, "f" node (i.e. contextually non-bound sentence item) in 49%, see Figure 3.

The particular "c", "t" and "f" node types are not distributed with the same frequency in the PDT, see Table 2 reflecting the ratio of occurrences of particular node types in the data (the PDT contains 354,841 contextually non-bound nodes ("f"), 176,225 non-contrastive contextually bound nodes ("t") and 30,312 contrastive contextually bound nodes ("c")).

Table 2: The PDT distribution of "f", "t" and "c" interconnected with a text coreference relation

%	f (from)	t (from)	c (from)
f (to)	5.52	11.55	9.09
t (to)	2.25	15.38	5.81
c (to)	0.65	2.08	3.52

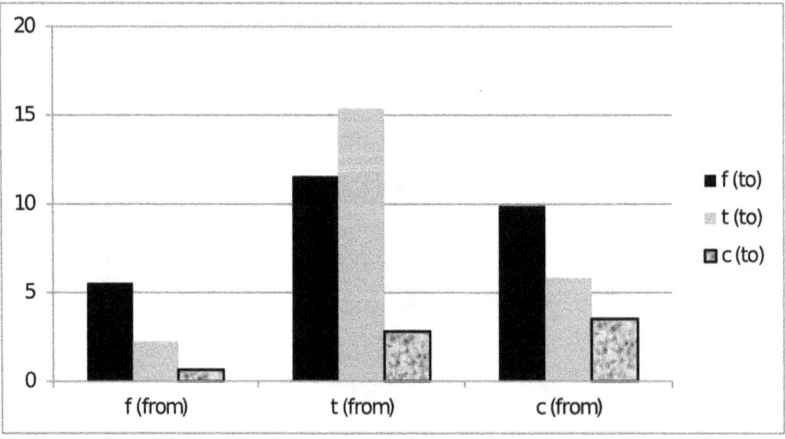

Figure 4: The PDT distribution of "f", "t" and "c" interconnected with a text coreference relation

3 Text coherence in the PDT

The contextually bound nodes ("t" and "c" nodes) generally have higher probability that the text coreference arrow will lead from them and also to them than contextually non-bound nodes ("f" nodes). Based on this, the most typical text coreference connection leads from a non-contrastive contextually bound node to another non-contrastive contextually bound node (i.e. from "t" to "t"), see (2) in §3.3. The second most typical text coreference connection leads from a non-contrastive contextually bound node to a contextually non-bound node (i.e. from "t" to "f"). The third most typical text coreference connection leads from a contrastive contextually bound node to a contextually non-bound node (from "c" to "f"). Generally, the most favored "starting" position for a text coreference arrow is a non-contrastive contextually bound sentence item ("t").

Table 3: Percentage of all "f" or "t+c" nodes interlinked with a text coreference relation in the PDT

%	(from)	t+c (from)
f (to)	5.52	11.19
t+c (to)	2.90	16.27

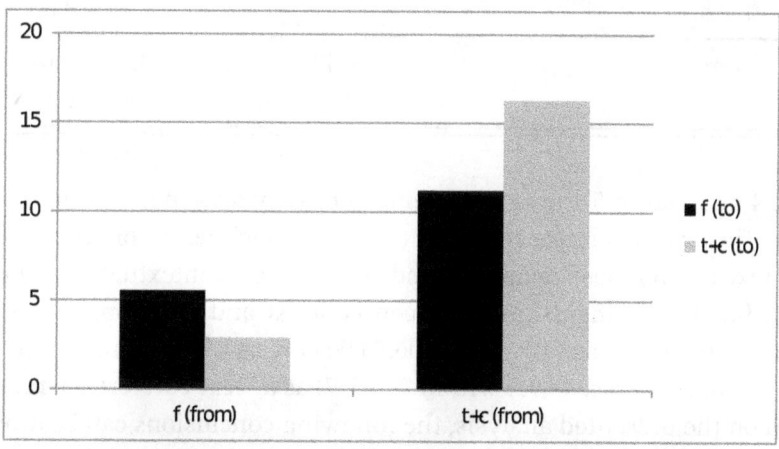

Figure 5: Percentage of all "f" or "t+c" nodes interlinked with a text coreference relation in the PDT

Contextually bound sentence items (both contrastive and non-contrastive that are mostly part of sentence Topic) are interlinked with text coreference relations more often than contextually non-bound (i.e. from the context non-deducible) items that are mostly part of sentence Focus, see Table 3 and Figure 5. Thus, the two described language phenomena, text coreference and sentence information structure, mutually cooperate in building the text coherence.

The individual node types differ in the fact where they find their parts of coreference chains. While the non-contrastive contextually bound nodes ("t") most likely are interconnected with contextually bound nodes, the contextually non-bound nodes ("f") mostly interconnected with contextually non-bound nodes (in terms of text coreference). The contrastive contextually bound nodes stand between these two tendencies – they are connected both with contextually bound and non-bound nodes (in relatively equal way). Such inclinations also demonstrate that it is worth distinguishing two different kinds of contextually bound nodes (contrastive and non-contrastive) because they contribute to the text coherence in different ways.

The individual node types ("t", "c" and "f") have in common that they all refer to the contrastive contextually bound nodes ("c") in the slightest degree (among them, the "c" nodes have the highest tendency to be interlinked with other "c" nodes).

Table 4: Percentage of "f", "t", "c" or "t+c" nodes interlinked with a text coreference relation in the PDT

%	f	t	c	t+c
from	8.42	29.02	18.42	27.46
to	12.03	20.91	23.29	21.26

Table 4 and Figure 5 shows a percentage of bound vs. non-bound nodes participating in text coherence relations (either as "recipients" or "senders"). The biggest text coreference "recipient" and "sender" are contextually bound nodes (without further distinguishing between contrast and non-contrast) – 27.46 % within all of them (i.e. 56,717 within 206,537) serve as a "text coreference sender" and 21.26 % of them (i.e. 43,911 within 206,537) as a "text coreference recipient".

Based on the presented analysis, the following conclusions can be drawn:

- Generally, a text coreference arrow (i) starts in every 5th–6th and leads to every 4th contrastive contextually bound sentence item ("c" node);
(ii) starts in every 3rd–4th and to every 5th non-contrastive contextually bound sentence item ("t" node) and (iii) starts in every 12th and to every 8th contextually non-bound sentence item ("f" node).

3 Text coherence in the PDT

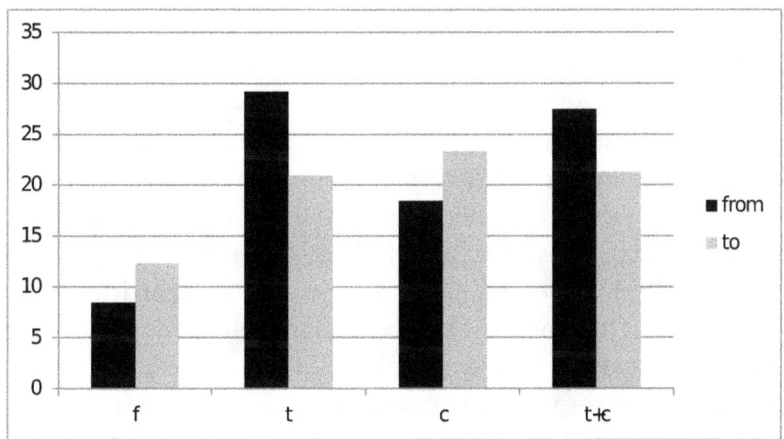

Figure 6: Percentage of "f", "t", "c" or "t+c" nodes interlinked with a text coreference relation in the PDT

- The contextually non-bound nodes ("f") as well as contrastive contextually bound ("c") nodes serve more often as text coreference "recipient" than "sender".

- Conversely, the non-contrastive contextually bound nodes ("t") serve more often as a text coreference "sender" than "recipient".

5 Conclusions

The paper has examined the correlation between sentence information structure and text coreference on the data of the Prague Dependency Treebank. Altogether, the PDT contains 86,590 text coreference relations interconnecting contextually bound or non-bound sentence items. The analysis shows that the text coreference relations operate rather within contextually bound nodes, i.e. if a sentence item is contextually bound (in terms of sentence information structure), it has a relatively high probability to be interconnected with another sentence item in a text coreference relation.

On the other hand, there is also a relatively significant part of contextually non-bound sentence items interconnected with another part of text through text coreference. The text coreference arrow leads from every 12th contextually non-bound sentence item ("f" node). It means that every 12th contextually non-bound sentence item clearly refers to the previous language context (in terms of text coreference). However, these two facts are not in contradiction. It is well known that entities mentioned in the previous text can be used in a new perspective (i.e. as contextually non-bound items) and they can bring new and unknown information to the text addressee (cf. *Do you want tea or coffee? – Tea, please.*).

In this context, contextually bound sentence items cannot be defined simply as coreferentially referring to the previous language context. They refer to the previous text (through text coreference) clearly more often than the contextually non-bound items. However, such kind of text referring is also not rare – according to the PDT, the contextually non-bound items participate in the text coreference in about 35%, non-contrastive contextually bound items in 60% and contrastive contextually bound items in 5%.

In this respect, the corpus-based research also demonstrates that the annotation of text coreference cannot be (without further specification) a reliable basis for the automatic annotation of sentence information structure in large corpora. If every sentence item annotated as referring to the previous context (in terms of text coreference) were automatically annotated also as contextually bound, it would constitute a large degree of error (based on the data from the PDT, the error rate would be about 35%).

Acknowledgments

The author acknowledges support from the Ministry of Culture of the Czech Republic (project n. DG16P02B016 *Automatic Evaluation of Text Coherence in Czech*). This work has been using language resources developed, stored and distributed by the LINDAT/CLARIN project of the Ministry of Education, Youth and Sports of the Czech Republic (project LM2015071).

References

Ariel, Mira. 1988. Referring and accessibility. *Journal of Linguistics* 24(01). 65–87.
Bejček, Eduard, Eva Hajičová, Jan Hajič, Pavlína Jínová, Václava Kettnerová, Veronika Kolářová, Marie Mikulová, Jiří Mírovský, Anna Nedoluzhko, Jarmila Panevová, Lucie Poláková, Magda Ševčíková, Jan Štěpánek & Šárka Zikánová. 2013. *Prague Dependency Treebank 3.0.* Prague, Czech Republic: Univerzita Karlova v Praze, MFF, ÚFAL. http://ufal.mff.cuni.cz/pdt3.0/.

Chiarcos, Christian. 2014. Towards interoperable discourse annotation. Discourse features in the ontologies of linguistic annotation. In Nicoletta Calzolari, Khalid Choukri, Thierry Declerck, Hrafn Loftsson, Bente Maegaard, Joseph Mariani, Asuncion Moreno, Jan Odijk & Stelios Piperidis (eds.), *Proceedings of the Ninth International Conference on Language Resources and Evaluation (LREC'14)*, 4569–4577. Reykjavik, Iceland: European Language Resources Association (ELRA).

Eckert, Miriam & Michael Strube. 2000. Dialogue acts, synchronizing units, and anaphora resolution. *Journal of Semantics* 17(1). 51–89.

Grosz, Barbara J. & Candace L. Sidner. 1986. Attention, intentions, and the structure of discourse. *Computational Linguistics* 12(3). 175–204.

Hajičová, Eva, Barbara Partee & Petr Sgall. 1998. *Topic-focus articulation, tripartite structures, and semantic content.* Vol. 71. Dordrecht: Kluwer.

Hajičová, Eva. 2011. On interplay of information structure, anaphoric links and discourse relations. In. *Societas Linguistica Europaea, SLE 2011 – 44th Annual Meeting.* Javier Martin Arista (ed.). Universidad de La Rioja. 139–140.

Hajičová, Eva, Barbora Hladká & Lucie Kučová. 2006. An annotated corpus as a test bed for discourse structure analysis. In *Proceedings of the Workshop on Constraints in Discourse*, 82–89. Maynooth, Ireland: National University of Ireland.

Joshi, Aravind K. & Scott Weinstein. 1981. Control of inference: Role of Some aspects of discourse Structure-Centering. In *IJCAI*, 385–387.

Komen, Erwin R. 2012. Coreferenced corpora for information structure research. Studies in Variation, Contacts and Change in English (10).

Nedoluzhko, Anna. 2011. *Rozšířená textová koreference a asociační anafora (Koncepce anotace českých dat v Pražském závislostním korpusu)* (Studies in Computational and Theoretical Linguistics). Praha, Česká Republika: Ústav formální a aplikované lingvistiky.

Nedoluzhko, Anna. 2015. Contextually Bound Expressions without a Coreference Link. In Zikánová, Šárka, Eva Hajičová, Barbora Hladká, Pavlína Jínová, Jiří Mírovský, Anna Nedoluzhko, Lucie Poláková, Kateřina Rysová, Magdaléna Rysová & Jan Václ. *Discourse and Coherence. From the Sentence Structure to Relations in Text.* (Studies in Computational and Theoretical Linguistics). Prague, Czechia: UFAL. 199–215.

Nedoluzhko, Anna & Eva Hajičová. 2015. Information structure and anaphoric links – a case study and probe. In *Corpus Linguistics 2015. Abstract book*, 252–254. Lancaster University, UK. Lancaster, UK: UCREL.

Pajas, Petr & Jan Štěpánek. 2008. Recent advances in a Feature-Rich framework for treebank annotation. In Donia Scott & Hans Uszkoreit (eds.), *The 22nd International Conference on Computational Linguistics – Proceedings of the Conference*, vol. 2, 673–680. Manchester, UK: The Coling 2008 Organizing Committee.

Rysová, Kateřina & Magdaléna Rysová. 2015. Analyzing text coherence via multiple annotation in the Prague Dependency Treebank. In Pavel Král & Václav Matoušek (eds.), *Text, Speech, and Dialogue: 18th International Conference, TSD 2015* (Lecture Notes in Artificial Intelligence 9302), 71–79. University of West Bohemia. New York: Springer International Publishing.

Rysová, Kateřina, Magdaléna Rysová & Eva Hajičová. 2015. *Topic–focus articulation in English texts on the basis of Functional Generative Description*. Tech. rep. TR 2015-59. Prague, Czechia.

Sgall, Petr. 1967. *Generativní popis jazyka a česká deklinace*. Prague, Czech Republic: Academia.

Stede, Manfred & Arne Neumann. 2014. Potsdam Commentary Corpus 2.0: Annotation for Discourse Research. In Nicoletta Calzolari, Khalid Choukri, Thierry Declerck, Hrafn Loftsson, Bente Maegaard, Joseph Mariani, Asuncion Moreno, Jan Odijk & Stelios Piperidis (eds.), *Proceedings of the Ninth International Conference on Language Resources and Evaluation (LREC'14)*, 925–929. Reykjavik, Iceland: European Language Resources Association (ELRA). http://www.lrec-conf.org/proceedings/lrec2014/pdf/579_Paper.pdf.

Štěpánek, Jan & Petr Pajas. 2010. Querying diverse treebanks in a uniform way. In *Proceedings of the 7th International Conference on Language Resources and Evaluation (LREC 2010)*, 1828–1835. Valletta, Malta: European Language Resources Association.

Chapter 4

Applying computer-assisted coreferential analysis to a study of terminological variation in multilingual parallel corpora

Koen Kerremans

Vrije Universiteit Brussel

> Coreferential analysis involves identifying linguistic items (usually both lexical and grammatical items) that denote the same referent in a given text. To be able to study such coreferential items, each item first needs to be indexed or annotated according to a referent's corresponding identification code or label. Linguistic items that are identified as 'coreferential' can be represented in a coreferential chain, i.e. a list of coreferential items extracted from the text in which the order of the items in the text is retained. We will discuss some of the benefits of applying coreferential analysis to a study of intra- and interlingual terminological variation in multilingual parallel corpora. Intralingual terminological variation refers to the different ways in which specialised knowledge can be expressed by means of terminological units (both single and multiword units) in a collection of source texts. Interlingual variation pertains to the different ways in which these source language terms are translated into the languages of the target texts. In this contribution, I will focus on how the method of coreferential analysis was used in a comparative study of (intra- and interlingual) terminological variation in original texts (i.e. the source texts) and their translations (i.e. the target texts). I will present a semi-automatic method to support the manual identification of intralingual terminological variants based on coreferential analysis. We will discuss how data resulting from coreferential analysis can be used to quantitatively compare terminological variation in source and target texts. Finally, I will present a new type of translation resource in which terminological variants in the source language are represented as a network of coreferential links.

Koen Kerremans. 2017. Applying computer-assisted coreferential analysis to a study of terminological variation in multilingual parallel corpora. In Katrin Menzel, Ekaterina Lapshinova-Koltunski & Kerstin Kunz (eds.), *New perspectives on cohesion and coherence*, 45–68. Berlin: Language Science Press. DOI:10.5281/zenodo.814464

Koen Kerremans

1 Introduction

The work presented in this contribution further builds on a research study that focused on how terms and equivalents recorded in multilingual terminological databases can be extended with terminological variants and their translations retrieved from English source texts and their translations into French and Dutch (Kerremans 2012). First, a distinction needs to be made between intralingual (terminological) variation and interlingual variation. The former refers to different ways in which specialised knowledge can be expressed by means of terms in a collection of source texts. Interlingual variation pertains to a study of the different ways in which these source language terms were translated into the languages of the target texts.

In many terminology approaches, terminological variants within and across languages are identified on the basis of semantic and/or linguistic criteria (Carreño Cruz 2008; Fernández Silva 2010). Given the fact that the general aim of the study reported by Kerremans (2012) was to examine how and to what extent patterns of variation in source texts are reflected in the translations, I decided to apply coreferential analysis to the study of (intralingual) terminological variation in the source texts and contrastive analysis to the study of interlingual variation. Our approach based on these perspectives of analysis is motivated by the fact that in order to acquire an understanding about the unit of specialised knowledge or 'unit of understanding' (Temmerman 2000)[1] that needs to be translated, translators first analyse the different ways in which this unit is expressed in the source text, how its meaning is developed in the text (i.e. the textual perspective) and how it can be rendered in the target language (i.e. the contrastive perspective). The combination of coreferential and contrastive methods of analysis allows us to retrieve a list of terminological units for a preselected set of units of understanding in the source texts and to compare this list to the equivalents of each terminological unit in the target texts.

In text-linguistic approaches to the study of terminology (Collet 2004), it has been advocated that terms function as cohesive devices in a text in the sense that they contribute to the reader's general understanding of the text and, in particular, of the units of understanding (Temmerman 2000). As a result of this, the occurrence of terminological variants in a given text is also functional in the sense that these variants allow authors to express their different ways of 'looking' at the same units of understanding (Cabrè 2008; Freixa, Fernández Silva & Cabrè 2008; Fernández Silva 2010).

---

[1] In (Temmerman 2000), the term 'unit of understanding' is used instead of 'concept' to emphasise the prototypical structure of specialised knowledge.

4 Terminological variation in multilingual parallel corpora

Within text-linguistic studies, coreferential analysis is a method for linguistic analysis that is used to study patterns of cohesion in a text (Section 2). The purpose of this contribution is to discuss some of the benefits of applying coreferential analysis to a study of intra- and interlingual terminological variation in multilingual parallel corpora (Section 3). My focus will be on three topics in particular:

1. the possibility to support the process of identifying terminological variants as coreferential items by means of a semi-automatic method (see Section 4);

2. the possibility to carry out quantitative comparisons of terminological variants that are identified on the basis of coreferential analysis (see Section 5);

3. the possibility to create a new type of translation resource in which terminological variants in the source language are represented as a network of coreferential links (see Section 6).

By focusing on these three topics in particular, I hope to provide research ideas for future (quantitative and qualitative) studies adopting a textual perspective to terminological variation (see Section 7).

2 Research background

In this section, I want to make clear how terminological variation is defined in the present study (see Section 2.1). Given the fact that I adopt a textual perspective to the study of this phenomenon (see previous section), I want to briefly describe what this perspective involves and how coreferential analysis fits within this perspective (see Section 2.2).

2.1 Terminological variation as the object of study

A study of terminological variation can theoretically pertain to any set of terms in a domain's specialised discourse. In practice, boundaries will need to be drawn in order to limit the scope of the study to a scalable subset of data. According to Daille (2005), these boundaries can be determined by the potential use of the results of the study in various applications (e.g. information retrieval, machine-aided text indexing, scientific and technology watch and controlled terminology for computer-assisted translation systems), the computer techniques involved in studying the phenomenon and/or the types of language data (mono-/bi-/multilingual data). The application-oriented view explains why a definition of the phenomenon in one study of terminological variation cannot simply be applied to another study.

Based on a review of earlier studies of terminological variation, Cea & Montiel-Ponsoda (2012) present a typology of term variants that is based on a three-fold structure:

1. The first group encompasses a group of synonyms or terminological units that refer to an identical concept. The types of term variants that enter this group are graphical and orthographical variants (e.g. 'Kyoto-protocol' vs. 'Kyoto protocol'), inflectional variants (e.g. 'introduction' and 'introductions') or morpho-syntactic variants ('greenhouse gas emissions' and 'emissions of greenhouse gases').

2. The second group of variants covers partial synonyms or terminological units that highlight different aspects of the same concept. To this group belong stylistic or connotative variants (e.g. 'recession' vs. 'r-word'), diachronic variants (e.g. 'tuberculosis' and 'phthisis'), dialectical variants ('gasoline' vs. 'petrol'), pragmatic or register variants (e.g. 'swine flu' vs. 'pig flu' vs 'Mexican pandemic flu' vs. 'H1N1') and explicative variants ('immigration law' vs. 'law for regulating and controlling immigration'). Examples of these types have been studied in different fields (Temmerman 1997; Resche 2000; Fernández Silva 2010).

3. The third group of variants covers terminological units that show formal similarities but refer to different concepts Daille et al. (1996); Arlin et al. (2006); Bowker & Hawkins (2006); Depierre (2007). Examples are terms showing lexical similarities (e.g. 'Kyoto-protocol' vs. 'Kyoto mechanism') or morphological similarities (e.g. 'biodiversity' vs. 'biosphere' vs. 'biology').

In my study, terminological variation pertains to the first two groups of variants discussed by Cea & Montiel-Ponsoda (2012). It was stated earlier (see Section 1) that as far as intralingual terminological variation is concerned, I applied coreferential analysis to study this phenomenon in a collection of source texts. This implies a textual perspective to the study of terminological variation that I want to briefly discuss in the next section before I explain how the method of coreferential analysis was carried out in my study (see Section 3).

2.2 A textual perspective applied to terminological variation

Within the textual perspective, a distinction needs to be made between text coherence and text cohesion. Based on an extensive review of literature addressing these two topics, Tanskanen (2006: 7) notes that there is a general consensus to define cohesion and coherence as follows:

> "Cohesion refers to the grammatical and lexical elements on the surface of a text which can form connections between parts of the text. Coherence, on the other hand, resides not in the text, but is rather the outcome of a dialogue between the text and its listener or reader. Although cohesion and coherence can thus be kept separate, they are not mutually exclusive, since cohesive elements have a role to play in the dialogue."

Cohesion and coherence contribute to the general texture within a text. In other words, they are a set of characteristics that allows the text to function as a whole. Cohesion is generally regarded as a text internal property, whereas coherence is not. The latter can only be attributed to the text by the reader who is thought to use background knowledge during the interpretation process of the text. This allows the reader to create correlates between the text and the outside world. This knowledge "encompasses beliefs and assumptions about the world as well as language-related knowledge, i.e. knowledge about grammar and about words and their meanings but also knowledge about how texts function" (Collet 2004: 104). Given the fact that the focus of this study is on terminological variation in texts, I will only be concerned with text cohesion.

Cohesion as a text internal property is created on the basis of connected text fragments that allow meaning to pass from one text fragment to another, thus establishing cohesive chains within the text. Collet (2004) describes these as "chains of text fragments that refer to the same concrete or abstract reality" and "which can be obtained with grammatical and lexical means" (ibid.). Halliday & Hasan (1976) propose five types of cohesion: reference, substitution, ellipsis, conjunction and lexical cohesion. Since my study focuses on terms as cohesive devices in texts (see Section 1), I shall only focus on lexical cohesion.

Applied to studies of terminology, lexical cohesion analysis is achieved by means of a selection of a domain's terminology appearing in a text. Halliday & Hasan (1976) distinguish between two types of lexical cohesion: reiteration and collocation. They define the former as a form of lexical cohesion "which involves the repetition of a lexical item, at one end of the scale; the use of a general word to refer back to a lexical item, at the other end of the scale; and a number of things in between - the use of a synonym, near-synonym, or superordinate" (ibid.: 278). Collocation occurs between any pair of lexical items "that stand to each other in some recognizable lexico-semantic (word meaning) relation" (ibid: 285). In other words, the 'collocation' refers to "an associative meaning relationship between regularly co-occurring lexical items" (Tanskanen 2006: 12).

In the present study, terminological variation is clearly seen as the result of a process of reiteration whereby the author of a text uses the same or different terminological units to express the same unit of understanding. In this perspective, coreferential analysis is a technique that is suitable for identifying those linguistic items that refer to the same unit of understanding in a text. To be able to study such coreferential items, each item first needs to be indexed or annotated according to a referent's corresponding identification code or label. Linguistic items that are identified as 'coreferential' can be represented in a coreferential chain, i.e. a list of coreferential items extracted from the text in which the order of the items in the text is retained.

Rogers (2007) shows how the technique of coreferential analysis can be used to study patterns of terminological equivalence between source and target texts. By presenting terminological variants as coreferents in lexical chains she is able to compare the use of terms in establishing cohesive ties in a German technical text and its translations into English and French. Before I illustrate on the basis of examples from my own study how this method is carried out, I will first briefly present in the next section the research design of the case study presented by Kerremans (2012), which forms the basis for the present study. This will allow us to motivate the particular choices that were made with respect to the method of analysis.

3 Intra- and interlingual variation in parallel texts

The general aim of the study described in Kerremans (2012) was to try to understand how translators of specialised texts tend to deal with terminological variation in texts that need to be translated (i.e. source texts). For instance, a topic such as the rise in the average temperature of the earth's surface can be referred to in English as 'global warming', 'greenhouse effect' or 'hothouse effect'. By comparing such terms in English source texts with their translations in Dutch and French versions of these texts (i.e. target texts), the overall aim of this study was to acquire a better insight into various ways of translating English environmental terminology into Dutch and French.

4 Terminological variation in multilingual parallel corpora

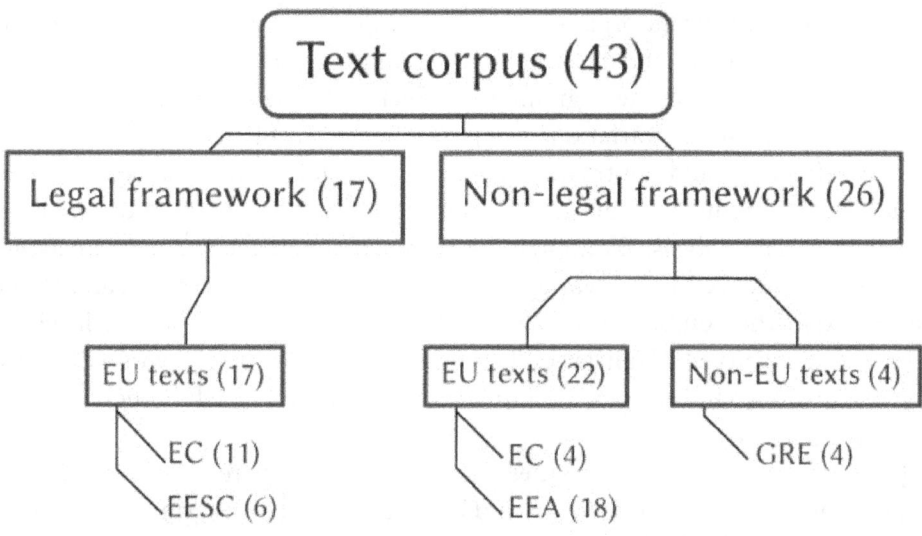

Figure 1: Classification of texts

The corpus created for this study is comprised of 43 texts. Each text is available in three language versions - English, French and Dutch - which means that in total 129 texts were used to study patterns of intra- and interlingual variation. All the texts in the corpus were originally written in English and translated into French and Dutch. The texts dealt with environmental topics, such as biodiversity loss, climate change, invasive species and environmental pollution. Texts were collected from different organisations (mainly EU institutions) and written registers (e.g. EU directives, information brochures, etc.) in order to study variation in relation to different situational parameters, such as text source, text framework (see Section 6). Figure 1 shows how the texts in the corpus were classified according to different text perspectives.

First of all, a distinction is made between 17 texts (69,647 words in the English versions) belonging to the legal framework (e.g. EC communications, green papers and staff working documents, EESC opinions) and 26 texts (39,183 words in the English versions) that do not belong to this framework (e.g. fact sheets and booklets). Within the first category, only EU texts were added to the corpus. Within the second category, a further distinction was made between 22 EU texts and 4 non-EU texts. Apart from these two text dimensions, texts were also classified according to the institution responsible for the trans-lation and publication of the texts: the European Economic and Social Committee (EESC), the European Commission (EC), the European Environment Agency (EEA) and, finally, Green-

55

facts (GRE), a non-profit organisation that summarises and translates scientific publications on health and environmental issues for the general public. [2]

As was mentioned in the beginning (see Section 1), the research data (i.e. both intra- and interlingual variation) were collected from this corpus by applying both coreferential and contrastive analyses. In total, approximately 9,100 terminological variants were extracted from the English source texts on the basis of coreferential analysis. By applying a contrastive perspective, the translation equivalents of these English variants were retrieved from the French and Dutch target texts. The combination of an English term and its translation in either French or Dutch (i.e. a Translation Unit or TU), is stored in a separate database. The result was a database of approximately 18,200 TUs (English-French; English-Dutch).

Quantitative comparisons of these translation units were carried out in subsequent phases of the project. Each TU is comprised of a term in the source language (i.e. English), its corresponding equivalent that was retrieved from the target text in combination with additional contextual information: i.e. a specification of the unit of understanding to which the source language term refers as well as information about specific properties of the text from which the TU was retrieved.

Given the fact that the focus of this contribution is on coreferential analysis, it will be briefly illustrated by means of the example in Figure 2 how this particular analysis was carried out.

The figure contains an annotation scheme featuring 10 cluster labels and a text sample taken from a European Commission Staff Working document (European Communities 2008: 2). Cluster labels are ad-hoc labels that were created to facilitate the annotation of English terminological variants as coreferential items. Each cluster label represents a particular unit of understanding (see Section 1). For instance, the cluster label INVASIVE_ALIEN_SPECIES represents the unit of understanding (or conceptual category) that can be described as 'species that enter a new habitat and threaten the endemic fauna and/or flora'. Terminological variants that are annotated according to this label will appear in the lexical chain or 'cluster' of terms denoting the same unit of understanding in the text (see Table 1). For instance, the lexical chain drawn from the text sample in Figure 2 for the unit of understanding INVASIVE_ALIEN_SPECIES is: invasive alien species – IAS – invasive species – IS – IS – IS – invader.

---

[2] Texts from the European Economic and Social Committee (EESC) and the Committee of the Regions (COR) were classified according to one category EESC because texts from both institutions are translated by the same translation department.

4 Terminological variation in multilingual parallel corpora

Annotation scheme	Text sample
ALIEN_SPECIES BIOCONTROL BIODIVERSITY BIO-INVASION ECOSYSTEM FORESTRY INTRODUCTION INVASIVE_ALIEN_SPECIES MEA SPREAD	[Invasive Alien Species]$_{INVASIVE\_ALIEN\_SPECIES}$" are [alien species]$_{ALIEN\_SPECIES}$ whose [introduction]$_{INTRODUCTION}$ and/or [spread]$_{SPREAD}$ threaten [biological diversity]$_{BIODIVERSITY}$ [...]. The [Millennium Ecosystem Assessment]$_{MEA}$ revealed that [IAS]$_{INVASIVE\_ALIEN\_SPECIES}$ impact on all [ecosystems]$_{ECOSYSTEM}$ [...]. The problem of [biological invasions]$_{BIO-INVASION}$ is growing rapidly as a result of increased trade activities. [Invasive species]$_{INVASIVE\_ALIEN\_SPECIES}$ ([IS]$_{INVASIVE\_ALIEN\_SPECIES}$) negatively affect [biodiversity]$_{BIODIVERSITY}$ [...]. [IS]$_{INVASIVE\_ALIEN\_SPECIES}$ can cause congestion in waterways, damage to [forestry]$_{FORESTRY}$, crops and buildings and damage in urban areas. The costs of preventing, controlling and/or eradicating [IS]$_{INVASIVE\_ALIEN\_SPECIES}$ and the environmental and economic damage are significant. The costs of [control]$_{BIOCONTROL}$, although lower than the costs of continued damage by the [invader]$_{INVASIVE\_ALIEN\_SPECIES}$, are often high.

Figure 2: Example illustrating coreferential analysis

Table 1: Results of the coreferential analysis

Cluster label	Lexical chain
INVASIVE_ALIEN_SPECIES	invasive alien species - IAS - Invasive species - IS - IS - IS - invader
ALIEN_SPECIES	alien species
INTRODUCTION	introduction
SPREAD	spread
BIODIVERSITY	biological diversity - biodiversity
MEA	Millennium Ecosystem Assessment
ECOSYSTEM	ecosystems
BIO-INVASION	biological invasions
FORESTRY	forestry
BIOCONTROL	control

Co-referential analysis focuses on reformulation procedures, which according to Ciapuscio (2003: 212), are procedures defined mainly on the basis of structural criteria, such as "the rewinding loop in speech, the resumption of an idea that has already been verbalized, which is linguistically realised in the two-part structure "referential expression" + "treatment expression", both expressions usually being linked with markers." The first term ('Invasive Alien Species') which introduces the unit of understanding INVASIVE_ALIEN_SPECIES in the text sample (see 2) is called the 'referential expression'. It represents the perspective from which the referent should be perceived. This is the reason why all coreferential expressions in Figure 2 are annotated according to the cluster label INVASIVE_ALIEN_SPECIES. The expressions that follow the referential expression are called treatment expressions because they reveal a new aspect of the referent. The choice for a particular cluster label is determined by the referential expression, not by the treatment expression. For instance, the term 'alien species' may be annotated as ALIEN_SPECIES or as INVASIVE_ALIEN_SPECIES, depending on whether the term occurs as referential expression or treatment expression (i.e. shortened form of the term invasive alien species).

Coreferential analysis in my study was guided by the following rules:

- Every term candidate had to be a nominal pattern in order to have a common basis for comparing intralingual variants. The focus on nominal patterns makes sense in the context of terminology work, in which "the predominance of nouns is an incontestable phenomenon" (Bae 2006: 19). According to L'Homme (2003: 404) this focus on nominal patterns can be justified by the fact that specialised knowledge is usually "represented by terms that refer to entities (concrete objects, substances, artifacts, animates, etc.), and that entities are linguistically expressed by nouns."

- Every term candidate that is part of a linguistic construction that refers to a different unit of understanding should not be annotated. For instance, even though the pattern 'alien species' occurs two times in the text sample in Figure 2, only the second occurrence is marked with the corresponding ALIEN_SPECIES. This is because in the first occurrence, the term is part of the linguistic pattern 'invasive alien species' which refers to the unit of understanding INVASIVE_ALIEN_SPECIES.

- Every term candidate that is not part of a linguistic construction that refers to a different unit of understanding should be annotated. This rule applied to term candidates that are not part of a nominal construction - such as

4 Terminological variation in multilingual parallel corpora

'invasive alien species', 'invasive species' or 'biological diversity' (see 2) - or term candidates that are part of a nominal construction that did not refer to a different unit of understanding in my dataset. The term candidate 'control', for instance, was annotated as 'BIOCONTROL'. The term candidate appears in the nominal construction 'the costs of control', which did not refer to a different unit of understanding in my study.

- Every article or pronoun preceding a term candidate should be left out. For instance, in the nominal constituent 'The Millennium Ecosystem Assessment' (see 2), the article preceding the term candidate was not taken up in the analysis.

- All term candidates that are linked to one another in the same nominal pattern by means of coordinating conjunctions should be annotated separately. For instance, the pattern 'introduction and/or spread' features two different units of understanding in my dataset: resp. INTRODUCTION and SPREAD. More complex patterns to annotate were conjunctive patterns featuring different modifiers linked to one head. Consider for instance the text string 'invasive and alien species' which comprises two term variants ('invasive species' and 'alien species') that should be classified according to two different clusters: INVASIVE_ALIEN_SPECIES and ALIEN_SPECIES. The second term candidate in this pattern (i.e. 'alien species') does not pose any problem. The occurrence can be immediately extracted from the text without any modifications required. The first term candidate (i.e. 'invasive species'), however, could not be directly extracted as it is interrupted by the conjunction word 'and' and the adjective 'alien'. To be able to annotate this term candidate as occurrence of the unit of understanding INVASIVE_-ALIEN_SPECIES and to add the correct form 'invasive species' to a separate database containing the research data, a distinction had to be made between occurrences and base forms. The occurrence refers to the English term variant as it appeared in the corpus. The base form is a 'cleaned' version of the occurrence in which possible irrelevant words in multiword terms are deleted. In the example of 'invasive and alien species', for instance, the base form of this pattern referring to the cluster INVASIVE_-ALIEN_SPECIES is 'invasive species'. It should be noted that results derived from the quantitative analyses of intra- and interlingual variants in the corpus are based on the comparisons of base forms only (Section 5).

In Section 1, I mentioned that the purpose of this article is to discuss some of the benefits of applying the aforementioned method to a study of terminological variation in multilingual parallel corpora. In the remainder of this contribution, I will focus on the possibility to support the manual effort by means of automated procedures (Section 4), the possibility to carry out quantitative comparison of terminological variants in lexical chains (see Section 5) and, finally, the possibility to create a new type of translation resource in which terminological variants in the source language are represented as a network of coreferential links (see Section 6).

4 Computer-assisted coreferential analysis

A major drawback of the method outlined above is the fact that it is very difficult to apply if the work is only carried out manually. During the coreferential analysis of the source texts, 241 cluster labels needed to be taken into consideration in our study. Given the fact that the process of annotating or 'labeling' terminological variants as 'coreferential' involves performing manual actions which are to a certain degree repetitive and predictable, I developed a semi-automatic method to support this labour-intensive process.

Before I outline this method, it should be noted that different approaches have been proposed for automatically extracting intralingual terminological variation from texts. Some approaches are based on the search for contexts that contain predefined sets of text-internal markers, called Knowledge Patterns or KPs. In literature, such patterns are often used to extract two term candidates linked by a specific semantic relation. For a survey of such approaches, see Auger & Barrière (2008). In other approaches, terminological variants are identified on the basis of distributional measures. The basic idea in these approaches is that the more distributionally similar two term candidates are, the more likely that they can be used interchangeably in linguistic contexts (Weeds & Marcu 2005; Rychlý & Kilgarriff 2007; Shimizu et al. 2008; Kazama et al. 2010). A major disadvantage of approaches based on distributional measures is the difficulty to understand the types of semantic relations (e.g. synonymy, hyperonymy, antonymy, etc.) that can be inferred from the resulting clusters of words or terms (Budanitsky & Hirst 2006; Heylen, Peirsman & Speelman 2008; Peirsman, Heylen & Speelman 2008).

In order to make sure that, for the preselected set of units of understanding, all English terminological variants and their translations into French and Dutch would be retrieved from the trilingual corpus (see Section 3), while retaining the order of appearance of each variant in the texts, I decided to support my manual coreferential and contrastive methods of analysis by means of automated procedures. This semi-automatic approach allows us to ensure completeness, accuracy and consistency in the data obtained. The automated procedures are implemented in a script that was written in the Perl programming language[3].

Given the scope of this study, I shall only focus on the computer-assisted method supporting the manual identification of coreferential terminological variants in the English source texts. The purpose of this method is threefold: (1) to support the identification of terminological variants that are coreferentially linked to a common unit of understanding, (2) to annotate these variants according to a common cluster label (see Section 3) and (3) to extract these variants from the text and store them as lexical chains in a separate database.

It should be noted that prior to this method, each source text in the corpus needs to be aligned with its corresponding text(s) in the target language(s). After that, the script developed to support coreferential analysis reads every text segment (usually corresponding with a sentence in the text) one after the other and carries out a number of tasks. For each term variant that is manually selected in a text segment, the script will first suggest possible matching cluster labels, based on term variants that were manually entered in a previous stage. If no matching clusters were found, the proper cluster label needs to be specified by the user.

After that, the new term variant and its corresponding cluster label are stored in a dataset of 'Clusters'. Whenever the term variant is found in the subsequent text segments, it is automatically identified as a term candidate and its corresponding cluster label is presented to the user. In case of term variants that are already 'known' to the system, the user simply needs to confirm or reject the suggestions made by the system.

The computer-assisted method relies on three resources during the analysis of coreferential terminological variants in the source texts: i.e. 'Clusters', 'Filtering rules' and a 'Dictionary' (see Figure 3).

The function of each resource is explained as follows:

- 'Clusters': a dataset of all the cluster labels (see above) and the term variants already encountered in previous texts. The dataset is used to automatically identify and cluster term variants that were previously encountered during coreferential analysis. This dataset continuously grows as more variants are retrieved from texts.

- 'Filtering rules': a list of rules comparable to a stoplist. It contains patterns that should be ignored during the search for term candidates. As the search for term candidates was case-insensitive, for instance, the term candidate 'IS' pointing to the unit of understanding INVASIVE_ALIEN_SPECIES,

---

[3] https://www.perl.org/

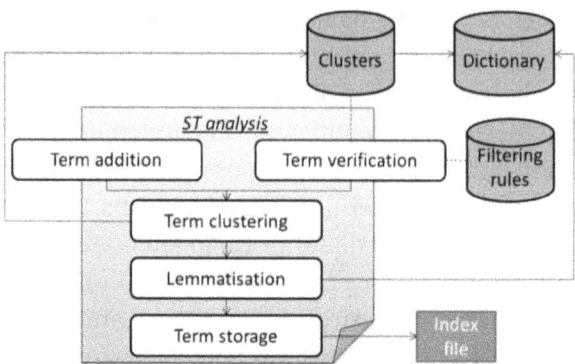

Figure 3: Computer-assisted coreferential analysis

more frequently occurred in the corpus as the third person singular of the verb 'to be'. Filtering rules specifying common patterns in which this form appears as a verb were necessary to exclude the irrelevant occurrences during the analysis of the source texts. Another example is for instance the term candidate 'community' referring to the unit of understanding BIOLOGICAL_COMMUNITY. Filtering rules were created to disregard occurrences of this string in patterns like 'scientific community' or 'economic community' which also frequently occurred in my corpus.

- 'Dictionary': a resource comprised of all occurrences retrieved from the source texts, together with their lemmatised forms. The distinction between lemmatised forms and actual occurrences was necessary to be able to deal with frequently encountered discontinuous multiword expressions such as the term 'control of invasive species' in the string 'control and prevention of invasive species'. Term occurrences were stored in the 'Clusters' dataset (see Figure 5), whereas lemmatised forms were stored in the dictionary.

The semi-automatic method is implemented in such a way that the three aforementioned resources are updated and expanded with new data, any time during the analysis. As a result, the time spent on manually extracting the lexical chains from the source texts is considerably reduced as the analysis proceeds.

Figure 3 also visualises the different semi-automated steps to add term variants to an index file, together with information about their position in the source text and their corresponding cluster labels. This index file is used in a later phase of the project to semi-automatically retrieve the translation equivalents from the aligned target texts. The semi-automated steps supporting coreferential analysis are:

- 'Term addition': a semi-automated process that can be broken down into the following steps: a) in every text segment, a new term variant is manually highlighted, b) candidates of cluster labels are automatically proposed in the 'Term clustering' procedure and c) the new term variant is automatically added to the 'Clusters' dataset.

- 'Term verification': a semi-automated process whereby text strings corresponding to term candidates in the dataset of 'Clusters' are automatically selected as term variants. After manual validation, potentially relevant cluster labels are looked up in the dataset of clusters on the basis of the 'Term clustering' procedure (see the next step).

- 'Term clustering': a semi-automated process for assigning a proper cluster label to an already familiar term variant. Candidates of cluster labels are automatically proposed based on fuzzy matching between the new term variant and the variants that are already present in the dataset of 'Clusters'. The proper cluster label is manually selected in case more than one cluster candidate was found. In case only one candidate is found, the automatically proposed cluster can either be manually approved or rejected. In case the term variant should be classified according to a cluster that was not proposed as candidate, this cluster is manually selected from the entire dataset of clusters, after which the 'Clusters' dataset and the 'Dictionary' are updated. Finally, candidates of cluster labels are automatically proposed based on fuzzy matching between the new term variant and the variant clusters (see the 'Lemmatisation' process).

- 'Lemmatisation': a semi-automated process for assigning the correct lemmatised form to a term candidate. Candidates of lemmatised forms are automatically proposed based on fuzzy matching between the new term and the existing lemmatised forms. Next, the proper lemmatised form is manually selected in case more than one candidate was found. In case only one candidate is found, the automatically proposed lemma can either be manually approved or rejected. A lemmatised form has to be manually created in case it does not appear in the dictionary. After this, the dataset of clusters and the dictionary are updated and the validated term is stored in the resulting research data file (see the 'Term storage' procedure).

- 'Term storage': i.e. a semi-automated process for storing the validated occurrences of semantically-structured SL term variants in the aforementioned index file (see above).

The computer-assisted approach proved to be an efficient working method for annotating variants in coreferential chains, especially given the high repetition of frequently occurring patterns in the corpus that needed to be marked with the same cluster labels. Based on this method, it was possible to compile a dataset of approximately 9,100 English term variants retrieved from the corpus of source texts and classified according to a predefined set of 241 cluster labels.

5 Quantitative comparisons

By comparing the lexical chains in the source language with the translations of these chains in French and Dutch that were retrieved from the target texts, it was possible to draw conclusions on the occurrence of intra- and interlingual variation in the corpus.

When studied at the level of the text, interlingual variation occurs when terms appearing in the lexical chains in the source text were not consistently translated into the target texts, such as is the case in the example in Table 2. It can be observed from this table that in the French chain, the terminological choices that were made in the English text are reflected. An exception, for instance, is the translation of the English term 'IAS', which appears in the French translation as the full form 'espèces exotiques envahissantes'.

Table 2: English lexical chain and its translation into French and Dutch

English chain	French translation	Dutch translation
invasive alien species	▶ espèce exotique	~ invasieve uitheemse soort (IUS)
IAS	▶ espèces exotiques envahissantes	~ IUS
invasive species	▶ espèce envahissante	~ invasieve soort
IS	▶ EE	~ IS
IS	▶ EE	~ IS
Invader	▶ Envahisseur	~ IS
invasive species	▶ espèces envahissantes	~ invasieve soort

4 Terminological variation in multilingual parallel corpora

Quantitative analyses were carried out on the basis of comparisons between the English lexical chains and their translations into French and Dutch. The aim of the quantitative comparisons was to examine to what extent the English lexical chains had an impact on the choices made in the target languages. In order to examine this, I compared the transitions between consecutive lemmatised forms in the different chains. The transition from one form to the other is marked as '0' to indicate that no change occurred (e.g. from 'IS' to 'IS'). Changes in transitions (such as from 'invasive alien species' to 'IAS') are marked by '1'. The result of this analysis is a sequence of the values '1' and '0', which allowed us to create a transition profile for each English lexical chain and its corresponding chain in French and Dutch.

The example in Table 3 shows part of the transition profile for the coreferential chain of INVASIVE_ALIEN_SPECIES in TextID 1 (see Section 3). The transition profile for the coreferential chain is: 1 1 1 0 1 1.

Table 3: Example of a transition profile

Order in the text	English base forms for INVASIVE_ALIEN_SPECIES	Transition
1	invasive alien species	New
2	IAS	1
3	invasive species	1
4	IS	1
5	IS	0
6	invader	1
7	invasive species	1
	Degree of change:	0,83

The first occurrence 'invasive alien species' is marked as the beginning of a new lexical chain ('New'). The second occurrence 'IAS' differs from the first. The first transition is therefore marked as '1'. The fourth transition is marked as '0' because no change occurred in the transition from occurrence 4 ('IS') to 5 ('IS').

The lexical chain features five changes in the transitions between consecutive lemmatised forms on a total of six transitions. By dividing the first number by the second, a degree of change can be created for each coreferential chain separately. This measure allows for a quantitative comparison of the coreferential patterns in the three languages.

In the example in Table 4, the degrees of change for both English and French are 0,83, whereas for Dutch the value is 0,67. A value close to 1 indicates a high degree of change in the chain, whereas a degree of '0' indicates consistency in the lemmatised forms[4] in the pattern.

Table 4: Quantitative comparison between chains

English lemmatised forms		French lemmatised forms		Dutch lemmatised forms	
invasive alien species	New	espèce exotique	New	invasief uitheems soort (IUS)	New
IAS	1	espèce exotique envahissant	1	IUS	1
invasive species	1	espèce envahissant	1	invasief soort	1
IS	1	EE	1	IS	1
IS	0	EE	0	IS	0
Invader	1	Envahisseur	1	IS	0
invasive species	1	espèce envahissant	1	invasief soort	1
	0,83		0,83		0,67

Once results of the coreferential profiles and the degrees of change were obtained, two methods were applied for comparing variation in the different languages: one method was based on comparisons of the transition patterns in the three languages, the other on examining possible correlations between the degrees of change (see further).

The results in the first method of comparison were classified according to two possible 'scenarios': either the value was '0' (indicating no change in the transition) or '1' (indicating a change). General results are shown in Figure 4.

In 5,359 of the English cases, no variation was encountered in the transition between lemmatised forms in a chain. This corresponds to 72% of the total cases (n=7,446). A closer examination of this category shows that this pattern of consistency is also reflected in the translations. For instance, for the total set of chains,

---

[4] Note that each word in a term was lemmatised. In some cases, the lemmatisation of words resulted in multiword terms which were ungrammatical (e.g. *'espèce exotique envahissant' in French or *'invasief uitheems soort' in Dutch). This was necessary to make sure that variation resulting from morphological differences could be excluded from my analysis.

4 Terminological variation in multilingual parallel corpora

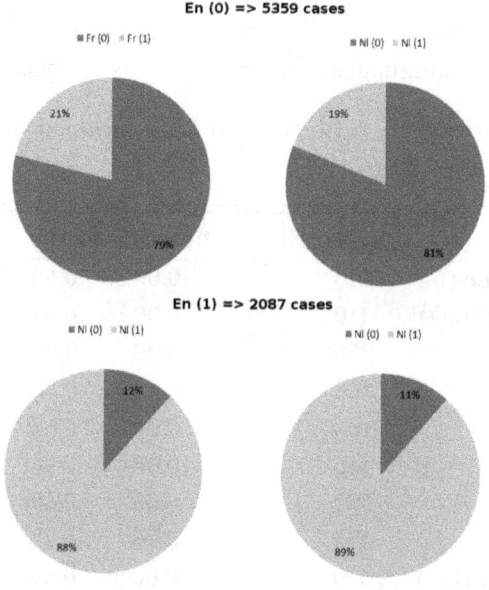

Figure 4: Comparisons of transition patterns

78% of the French cases and 81% of the Dutch cases follow the same pattern as English.

A closer look at the cases that were marked in English as '1' (2,087 cases or 28% of the total cases) shows that the transformations between lemmatised forms in Dutch and French also tend to be marked by this value: 88% of the French cases and 89% of the Dutch cases correspond to the English pattern.

Although these results already give an indication that variation in English coreferential chains is also reflected in the target languages, these results do not show to what extent the degree of variation within a coreferential chain is also reflected in the translations. In the first method, patterns of transition in the three languages are compared on a case by case basis, without taking into consideration the coreferential chain in which the transition takes place.

For this reason, a second type of quantitative comparison was worked out in which the aforementioned degree of variation within each chain was used as a basis for comparison. Given the general hypothesis that the source language has an impact on the choices made in the target language(s), it was hypothesised that the degree of changes in the English coreferential chains would also have a direct impact on the degree of changes in the French and Dutch chains. A bivariate analysis was conducted in PSPP[5], a free statistical software package, for all subsets in the corpus to determine possible correlations between the degrees of change in the three languages. The results of this analysis are shown in Table 5.

Table 5: Correlations between degrees of variation in coreferential chains

	N	Sig. (1- tailed)	En-Fr	En-Nl
EC (Leg)	456	0.00	0.66	0.61
EC (NLeg)	110	0.00	0.69	0.69
EEA	256	0.00	0.80	0.69
EESC	106	0.00	0.80	0.56
GRE	106	0.00	0.63	0.58
EU	366	0.00	0.76	0.69
Leg	562	0.00	0.69	0.60
Nleg	472	0.00	0.73	0.67
NLeg (EU)	110	0.00	0.69	0.69
Total	1034		0.71	0.63

Positive correlations can be observed in all datasets. The correlations between English and French tend to be stronger than those between English and Dutch. This is particularly the case in the EESC subset which shows a strong correlation between English and French (0,80) and a moderate correlation between English and Dutch (0,56).

6 Coreferential links in a dictionary application

In the previous section, I have shown how results that were partly derived from coreferential analysis can be used for research purposes only, i.e. to compare patterns of variation between source and target texts. In this section, I briefly show how coreferential links can also be used for visualising the relations between intralingual variants in a dictionary application. An example of a prototype visualisation is shown in Figure 5.

The model underlying the representation of variation in Figure 3 is based on the Hallidayan premise that each choice (variant) in a language system acquires its meaning against the background of other choices which could have been made.

---

[5] http://www.gnu.org/software/pspp/

4 Terminological variation in multilingual parallel corpora

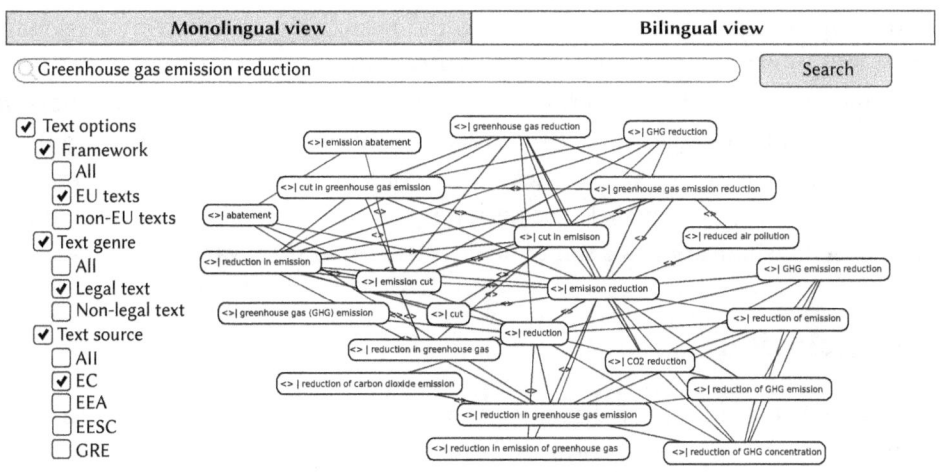

Figure 5: Coreferential links between terminological variants denoting
GREENHOUSE_GAS_EMISSION_REDUCTION

These choices are motivated by a complex set of contextual factors which, in Systemic Functional Linguistics, are classified according to the dimensions of Domain, Tenor and Mode (Eggins 2004).

Changing the contextual conditions or options in the model leads to direct changes in the network of terminological options that are shown to the user. Figure 5 shows a network of linguistic (terminological) options for the unit of understanding GREENHOUSE_GAS_EMISSION_REDUCTION in the source language. This network is activated by entering either a SL term appearing in the cluster or the specific cluster label in the search box (at the top). The search query will activate a number of contextual options that are associated with the search. It will also show the results of the search in a graph representation.

Connections in this graph represent the coreferential links between terms appearing in the same texts in the corpus. Selecting or deselecting one or several contextual or linguistic options in the filtering options, will immediately be reflected at the visualisation level. Examples of contextual options in Figure 5 are text options such as those that were mentioned in Section 3 (e.g. text source).

An additional interesting aspect of the graph representation is that it allows for a prototypically-structured visualisation of term variants referring to the same unit of understanding. This means that terms that frequently occurred in all texts have a lot of coreferential connections to other terms in the network. Consequently, these terms will take up a more central position in the network whereas infrequent patterns will appear more in the periphery. In this way, dictionary users will immediately be able to distinguish between 'core variants' (i.e. variants that are frequently encountered within the selected collection of texts) and 'peripheral variants' (i.e. variants that were only sporadically encountered). Selecting or deselecting certain contextual options can potentially cause term variants to move from the centre to the periphery or vice versa, allowing for dynamic, customised visualisations of semantically-structured term variants.

7 Conclusion

In this contribution, I have discussed how coreferential analysis can be used to identify term variants in a corpus of source texts, how the method can be supported by implementing semi-automatic procedures, how lexical chains in the source language and their translations can form the basis for quantitative comparisons between source and target texts and, finally, how coreferential links between intralingual variants can be represented in a dictionary application.

Coreferential chains can give us more insight in possible patterns of convergence or divergence among language versions of the same document. I therefore intend to further examine cohesive patterns in source and target texts for different reasons. For instance, it can be expected that differences in cohesive patterns will emerge if coreferential analysis is applied to all language versions (instead of the drafted versions only). By comparing the resulting coreferential chains in the different languages, it should be possible to calculate to what extent the target language versions deviate from the source texts in terms of terminological consistency and coreferential patterning. This is for instance valuable information for translators of EU legislation who have to see to it that no deviations occur in language versions of legally-binding texts. Differences in cohesive patterns are thus a possible method for further exploring the notion of anisomorphism in the context of EU translation. Anisomorphism refers to asymmetry in the interlinguistic transfer process, what González-Jover & Gómez (2006: 215) refers to as "the losses and gains that always occur in interlinguistic transfer processes, and which may be taken into account when comparing two different language systems."

Focusing on the coreferential chains in the target language versions will enable us to establish a new type of connection between 'linguistic options' in the source text (not based on the coreferential status of terms in a text but derived from translation similarities). For instance, the English expression 'climate risk' in TextID 6 (see Section 3) was not marked as part of the cluster CLIMATE_IM-

PACT. However, given the fact that in the French text this term was translated as 'conséquences du changement climatique' ('consequences of climate change'), which also appeared in the corpus as the translation of 'climate change impact', a link may be established between the term 'climate risk' and the English cluster of terms denoting CLIMATE_IMPACT:

> *English co-text:* "[...] *ensuring that long-term infrastructure will be proof to future* >>*climate risks*<< [...]"
>
> *French co-text:* "[...] *soient capables de résister aux* >>*conséquences du changement climatique*<< [...]"

Another example in the same text is the English term 'climate-resilient'. This term was not taken up in the cluster CLIMATE_ADAPTATION during the source text analysis but may be linked to this cluster on the basis of its French translation 's'adapter au changement climatique' ('to adapt to climate change')

> *English co-text:* "[...] *targeted action is needed on building codes and methods, and* >>*climate-resilient*<< *crops* [...]"
>
> *French co-text:* "[...] *l'élaboration de codes et de méthodes ainsi que la mise en place de cultures pouvant* >>*s'adapter au changement climatique*<< [...]"

Although my method proved to be valid for comparing patterns of variation, the time spent in this project on the method of analysis remains a major drawback. Fully automated extraction methods were not used, given the specific research requirements of data accuracy and completeness to be able to compare patterns of variation between the source and target texts. But since the work was characterised by a lot of repetitive tasks (such as selecting and annotating term variants that were previously encountered and thus already known) a combination of automatic procedures and manual verification proved to be efficient. Still, further reflections are necessary to conduct coreferential analyses in a way which seem more efficient and practical from a user perspective. For instance, it will need to be examined how the manual analysis can benefit from an automated co-referential resolution module.

Acknowledgements

The author wishes to thank the reviewers for their valuable comments on an earlier draft.

References

Arlin, Nathalie, Amélie Depierre, Susanne Lervad & Claire Rougemont. 2006. Réflexions sur la variation: étude de cas dans le domaine médical. *LSP and Professional Communication* 6(2). 75–88.

Auger, Alain & Caroline Barrière. 2008. Pattern-based approaches to semantic relation extraction: A state-of-the-art. *Terminology* 14(1). 1–19.

Bae, Hee Sook. 2006. Termes adjectivaux en corpus médical coréen: Repérage et désambiguïsation. *Terminology* 12(1). 19–50.

Bowker, Lynne & Shane Hawkins. 2006. Variation in the organization of medical terms: Exploring some motivations for term choice. *Terminology* 12(1). 79–110. http://www.benjamins.com/cgi-bin/t_articles.cgi?bookid=TERM%2012%3A1&artid=7060931, accessed 2008-03-10.

Budanitsky, Alexander & Graeme Hirst. 2006. Evaluating WordNet-based Measures of Lexical Semantic Relatedness. *Computational Linguistics* 32(1). Cited by 0869, 13–47.

Cabrè, Maria Teresa. 2008. El principio de poliedricidad: La articulación de lo discursivo, lo cognitivo y lo lingüístico en terminología (i). *IBÉRICA* 16. 9–36.

Carreño Cruz, Sahara Iveth. 2008. Characterizing term variation on an English-Spanish parallel corpus. In *Proceedings of Multilingual and Comparative Perspectives in Specialised Language Resources*. Marrakech.

Cea, Guadalupe Aguado-de & Elena Montiel-Ponsoda. 2012. Term variants in ontologies. In *Proceedings of the 30th International Conference of AESLA*, 19–21. Lleida.

Ciapuscio, Guiomar E. 2003. Formulation and Reformulation Procedures in Verbal Interactions between Experts and (Semi-)laypersons. *Discourse Studies* 5(2). 207–233. DOI:10.1177/14614456030050002004

Collet, Tanja. 2004. Esquisse d'une nouvelle microstructure de dictionnaire spécialisé reflétant la variation en discours du terme syntagmatique. *Méta* 49(2). 247–263.

Daille, Béatrice. 2005. Variations and application-oriented terminology engineering. *Terminology* 11(1). 181–197.

Daille, Béatrice, Benoît Habert, Christian Jacquemin & Jean Royauté. 1996. Empirical observation of term variations and principles for their description. *Terminology* 3(2). 197–258.

Depierre, Amélie. 2007. Souvent HAEMA varie …: Les dérivés du grec HAEMA en anglais: étude de cas de variation. *Terminology* 13(2). 155–176. DOI:10.1075/term.13.2.03dep

Eggins, Suzanne. 2004. *Introduction to Systemic Functional Linguistics: 2nd Edition.* London: Continuum International Publishing Group.

European Communities, Commission of the. 2008. *Commission Staff Working Document - Annex to the Communication from the Commission to the Council, the European Parliament, the European Economic and Social Committee and the Committee of the Regions - Towards an EU strategy on invasive species.*

Fernández Silva, Sabela. 2010. *Variación terminológica y cognición. Factores cognitivos en la denominación del concepto especializado.* Barcelona: Universitat Pompeu Fabra PhD thesis.

Freixa, Judit, Sabela Fernández Silva & Maria Teresa Cabrè. 2008. La multiplicité des chemins dénominatifs. *Meta* 53 (4). 731–747.

González-Jover & Adelina Gómez. 2006. Meaning and anisomorphism in modern lexicography. *Terminology* 12(2). 215–234.

Halliday, Michael A. K. & Ruqaiya Hasan. 1976. *Cohesion in English.* London: Longman Publishing.

Heylen, Kris, Yves Peirsman & Dirk Speelman. 2008. Modelling Word Similarity: An Evaluation of Automatic Synonymy Extraction Algorithms. In *Proceedings of the Sixth International Language Resources and Evaluation (LREC'08)*, 3243–3249. Marrakech.

Kazama, Jun'ichi, Stijn De Saeger, Kow Kuroda, Masaki Murata & Kentaro Torisawa. 2010. A Bayesian Method for Robust Estimation of Distributional Similarities. In *Proceedings of the 48th Annual Meeting of the Association for Computational Linguistics*, 247–256. Uppsala, Sweden: Association for Computational Linguistics.

Kerremans, Koen. 2012. Translating terminological variation: The case of biodiversity terminology. In L. Zybatow, A. Petrova & M. Ustaszewski (eds.), *Translationswissenschaft: Alte und neue Arten der Translation in Theorie und Praxis* (Forum Translationswissenschaft 16), 71–77. Frankfurt am Main: Peter Lang Verlag.

L'Homme, Marie-Claude. 2003. Capturing the lexical structure in special subject fields with verbs and verbal derivatives: A model for specialized lexicography. *International Journal of Lexicography* 16. 403–422. DOI:doi:10.1093/ijl/16.4.403

Peirsman, Yves, Kris Heylen & Dirk Speelman. 2008. Putting things in order. First and second order context models for the calculation of semantic similarity. In *Proceedings of the 9th Journées internationales d'Analyse statistique des Données Textuelles (JADT 2008)*, 907–916. Lyon.

Resche, Catherine. 2000. Equivocal economic terms or terminology revisited. *Meta* 45(1). 158–173.

Rogers, Margaret. 2007. Terminological equivalence in technical translation: A problematic concept? *Synaps : fagspråk, kommunikasjon, kulturkunnskap* 20. 13–25.

Rychlý, Pavel & Adam Kilgarriff. 2007. An efficient algorithm for building a distributional thesaurus (and other Sketch Engine developments). In *Proceedings of the 45th Annual Meeting of the Association for Computational Linguistics Companion Volume Proceedings of the Demo and Poster Sessions*, 41–44. Prague, Czech Republic: Association for Computational Linguistics.

Shimizu, Nobuyuki, Masato Hagiwara, Yasuhiro Ogawa, Katsuhiko Toyama & Hiroshi Nakagawa. 2008. Metric learning for synonym acquisition. In *Proceedings of the 22nd International Conference on Computational Linguistics (Coling 2008)*, 793–800. Manchester, UK: Coling 2008 Organizing Committee.

Tanskanen, Sanna-Kaisa. 2006. *Collaborating Towards Coherence: Lexical Cohesion in English Discourse.* Amsterdam/Philadelphia: John Benjamins Publishing Company.

Temmerman, Rita. 1997. Questioning the univocity ideal. The difference between socio-cognitive terminology and traditional terminology. *Hermes* 18. 51–90.

Temmerman, Rita. 2000. *Towards new ways of terminology description: The sociocognitive-approach.* Amsterdam/Philadelphia: John Benjamins Publishing Company.

Weeds, Julie & Daniel Marcu. 2005. Co-occurrence retrieval: A flexible framework for lexical distributional similarity. *Computational Linguistics* 31(4). 439–475.

Chapter 5

Testing target text fluency: A machine learning approach to detecting syntactic translationese in English-Russian translation

Maria Kunilovskaya
University of Tyumen

Andrey Kutuzov
University of Oslo

> This research is aimed at the semi-automatic detection of divergences in sentence structures between Russian translated texts and non-translations. We focus our attention on atypical syntactic features of translations, because they have a greater negative impact on the overall textual quality than lexical translationese. Inadequate syntactic structures bring about various issues with target text fluency, which reduces readability and the reader's chances to get to the text message. From a procedural viewpoint, faulty syntax implies more post-editing effort.
>
> In the framework of this research, we reveal cases of syntactic translationese as dissimilarities between patterns of selected morphosyntactic and syntactic features (such as part of speech and sentence length) in the context of sentence boundaries observed in comparable monolingual corpora of learner translated and non-translated texts in Russian.
>
> To establish these syntactic differences we resort to a machine learning approach as opposed to the usual statistical significance analyses. To this end we employ models that predict unnatural sentence boundaries in translations and highlight factors that are responsible for their 'foreignness'.

Maria Kunilovskaya & Andrey Kutuzov

For the first stage of the experiment, we train a decision tree model to describe the contextual features of sentence boundaries in the reference corpus of Russian texts. At the second stage, we use the results of the first multifactorial analysis as indicators of learner translators' choices that run counter to the regularities of the standard language variety. The predictors and their combinations are evaluated as to their efficiency for this task. As a result we are able to extract translated sentences whose structure is atypical against Russian texts produced without the constraints of the translation process and which, therefore, can be tentatively considered less fluent. These sentences represent cases of translationese.

1 Introduction

This research is an attempt to use machine learning algorithms to identify cases of less-than-typical syntactic structures in learner translations (syntactic translationese). We aim at developing a robust methodology, which could be used to look into differences between standard Russian and its translated variety and to select the linguistic features that are best in signalling these contrasts. It can be used to test researchers' intuitions as to the tendencies in translational behaviour and provide data for contrastive analysis. Solutions to both tasks (establishing typical deviations from the reference corpus and describing them in terms of predictive linguistic features) are applicable in translator training (the purpose we are immediately after) and in designing machine translation systems to improve fluency.

Linguistic peculiarities of translations distinguishing them from original texts in the same language are described within corpus-based translation studies. Typical research in this domain is usually designed to test linguistic indicators that reveal some tendencies in translations and to disentangle various factors that can be associated with certain translational behaviour, including extralinguistic ones. The aim is to arrive at a clearer understanding of the motivations behind translators' linguistic choices. While this is a possible and tempting extension for current research we refrain from making explicit claims as to why specific patterns are observed in our data. We proceed without a specific "universal" hypothesis in mind, beyond the assumption that the two corpora are significantly different (the argument that has been supported in our previous research on the same data in Kutuzov & Kunilovskaya (2015). That said, we do rely on previous work in this strand of corpus-based translation studies in selecting linguistic indicators of syntactic translationese, making use of suggested ways to implement their detection computationally and provide tentative descriptions of detected tendencies in line with some of the well-known concepts within this theory.

5 Testing target text fluency

An important aspect of our task is its focus on syntactic properties of translations. On the one hand, it is due to the role of sentence structure in the overall textual efficiency, in how easily a text is processed by the reader, how effectively it gets its message across. It has been shown that both structural integrity, interpreted as cohesion, and conceptual and pragmatic connectivity of corresponding discourse units (coherence) can be affected if target language specific (i.e. natural and conventional) sentence patterns are compromised in translation (e.g. with regard to failure to split sentences in translation, see Ramm 2006; Solfjeld 2008; Fabricius-Hansen 1999; Gile 2008; with regard to cohesion means, see Kachroo 1984; Hatim & Mason 1990). On the other hand, syntactic features of texts are less obvious to the naked eye, but are particularly informative in comparing corpora. There is ample evidence from corpus linguistics that functional and grammatical properties of words and surface characteristics of sentences (number and types of discourse markers, number of conjunctions and finite verbs, PoS, sentence length), which are typically used to operationalise syntactic or stylistic features of texts, are useful for the whole range of similar comparative tasks (for detecting translationese, see Baroni & Bernardini 2005; Pastor et al. 2008; in learner language studies Hinkel 2001; in authorship attribution and stylometry van Halteren 2007 and in text classification Koppel, Argamon & Shimoni 2002).

To achieve our goal, we use a traditional monolingual comparable corpora set-up: we exploit genre-comparable sub-corpora of the Russian National Corpus (**RNC**) and the Russian Learner Translator Corpus (**RusLTC**). The former is a reference corpus, which contains arguably representative sample of Russian language used to model dependencies that are then tested on translated data, the latter contains student translations that are viewed as particularly suitable for this task. They provide a strong case of human-produced translationese, because novice translators are notorious for generating disfluent texts that stand out for carrying foreign-sounding unnatural wording and structures. The corpora are described in detail in Section 3.

Methodologically, we follow the ideas of **multifactorial comparative analysis** of corpus data implemented within a supervised machine-learning approach suggested by Gries & Deshors (2014). One of the important improvements on previously used methods discussed in this work consists in ensuring contextual comparability of the phenomena under study. We tried to identify syntactic differences between the same corpora in previous experiments (Kutuzov & Kunilovskaya 2015) using de-contextualised PoS n-grams, but, against intuitive expectations and extensive theoretical evidence, failed to come up with meaningful results. Therefore, we introduce sentence boundaries (**SB**) as a structural 'anchor' to avoid over-generalisations of de-contextualised lexical and PoS frequencies and to ensure comparability of these features. Sentence boundaries are also an important linear syntactic event, which is traditionally used to gauge a number of textual properties such as sentence length and structural complexity.

We treat sentence boundaries as a surface feature of text structure and define it as an orthographically marked position, at which a sentence ends. It is typically marked with one of the four punctuation marks (full stop, dots, exclamation, question mark) or their combinations, and followed by a space and a capital letter. Effectively, sentence boundaries mark-off more or less independent chunks of information to be processed successively, thus encoding procedural information that guides pragmatic inference as to whether two informational constituents should be interpreted as a whole or individually, and how each of them relates to the topic and the intentional structure of the discourse (Guzmán & Klin 2000; van Dijk 1976; Carston & Behrens 2007; Unger 2011).

A meaningful study of semantic and pragmatic processes involved with speakers' motivations to start a new sentence (i.e. the analysis of regularities behind text/discourse segmentation into sentences *per se*) requires consideration of high-level linguistic phenomena (such as discourse and information structure), which are well beyond the scope of the present study. Instead we offer an account of typical and unnatural combinations of surface linguistic features at sentence boundaries as indicative of syntactic translationese.

At the same time, revealing unnatural sequences at sentence boundaries and sentences with atypical properties in Russian translations (in the present study limited to translations out of English) is potentially predictive of problematic text cohesion. Unlike English, non-emphatic Russian relies on word order as a primary means of structuring information. It has a strong tendency to place rhematic, new or focused elements in the sentence-final position (Grenoble 1998). This typological difference between the two language systems gives rise to the well-known structural deficiency of learner translations attributed to interference: they often contain prepositional phrases, which lack logical stress, at the end of the sentence (such as *никогда не слышал о нем* 'never heard of him'; *покарает его за это* 'will punish him for it'; *не успел избавиться от них* 'didn't have time to get rid of them' and adverbials (*купить по дешевке в России* 'to buy on the cheap in Russia').

The importance of maintaining cohesion in translation in ways licensed by the target language can hardly be overestimated. It was repeatedly stressed in translation studies (Blum-Kulka 1986; Hatim & Mason 2005; Baker 2011) on the grounds that faulty information structure and cohesion inadequacies can give rise to extra processing efforts for the reader entailed by the necessity to handle inconsistencies in co-reference, they and also lead to inappropriate topicalisations and induce misleading interpretations of either content or the speaker's intentions. This claim is corroborated by psycholinguistic research, which finds that during text processing 'due to limited attentional resources, precedence may be given to processes involved in building a locally coherent representation [...] there may not be sufficient resources left for more global processes, such as integrating the current sentence with information from earlier in the passage' (Guzmán & Klin 2000: 728). The recent trend in statistical machine translation and natural language generation research seeks to enrich existing architectures with text-level linguistic data in attempt to overcome their cohesion and coherence limitations (Meyer & Popescu-Belis 2012). So, current research can yield useful comparative information to be applied in translation quality assessment and machine translation as well as provide insights on cross-linguistic contrasts and translator behaviour. Teaching translator trainees about typical translational choices that deviate from standard language can be a useful consciousness-raising exercise, while linguistic indicators of possible translationese can be used to develop tools to range translations by the degree of their 'nativeness'.

The rest of the paper is structured as follows. Section 2 offers a brief overview of research on translation universals (it seems that this term is well-established in the field despite its limitations and will be used as such further on), especially at the level of syntax and in the area of methodology, while Section 3 introduces multidimensional analysis as our primary approach, describes our corpus data and comments on the principles and process of feature selection. It is followed by the empirical results in Section 4, where we report, compare and interpret the performance scores of the first-step model on both corpora. This part of the paper also describes how these results are used to train the second model, which effectively predicts errors of the first model, i.e. strong cases of syntactic dissonance with the reference corpus as well as informs of the linguistic features associated with them. In Section 5, we interpret our findings trying to isolate patterns that can be explained from contrastive and translational perspectives and present some considerations on model-fitting for future work. Section 6 concludes the work with some general considerations of its applicability and scalability in terms of accommodating more sophisticated features and their combinations to target higher-level linguistic phenomena.

2 Related work

As stated above, our research is set in the framework of the so called **translation universals theory**, which posits that translations differ from non-translations in the same language in a number of statistically measurable ways, while bearing some common features regardless of the source language. It focuses on empirically assessable properties of translated language known as *translationese* or *third code*, which are allegedly manifestations of *translation universals* or laws of translation. Without going into terminological details and the history of this paradigm of contemporary translation studies, now well-established, we merely outline main concepts of this approach and survey some studies that deal with the syntactic indicators of translationese and ways of their computational implementations.

Over the last 20 years or so research in this area has thrown up about a dozen of hypotheses about translational behaviour and a number of linguistic indicators to validate them. The most widely discussed tendencies include explicitation, interference and transfer, standardization (or levelling-out), simplification, normalisation, atypical patterning and over- and under-use of items. Most of these features can be revealed both at lexical and syntactic levels (Zanettin 2013).

In terms of methodology the study of universals is closely related to the Contrastive Interlanguage Analysis described in seminal works by Sylviane Granger (Granger 2010; Štěpánek & Pajas 2010). It can be built around either of three types of comparisons, surveyed in several papers, including Chesterman (2010) and Xiao, He & Yue (2010), or a combination thereof (i.e. on data from complex multi-corpora architectures, which enables the researcher to account for several factors simultaneously like in Pastor et al. (2008); Hansen-Schirra (2011); Dai & Xiao (2011); Bernardini (2007));

1. It can be based on monolingual comparable corpora and compare translations to non-translations in the same language (e.g. Laviosa (1998); Olohan (2001); Xiao, He & Yue (2010));

2. a less common approach is taken in Rayson et al. (2008), where lexical translationese is revealed as difference between texts translated by Chinese translators into English and versions of the same texts hand-corrected by English native speakers;

3. research into universals can require a parallel corpus component to reveal similarities and differences between sources and their translations (see an

almost unique research based on multiple parallel corpus in Castagnoli 2011);

4. finally, translations can be compared to translations into other languages or genres or by different translators (Baker 2004, among others).

Our research draws upon the results obtained in the pioneering work by Baroni & Bernardini (2005), who apply machine learning based on text classification to detect translationese. Their results are inspiring: they find that one can computationally learn the difference between high quality translations and very comparable non-translations by relying on distributions of some classes of function words. They also found out that humans are outperformed by machines in their ability to tell translations from non-translated language (Baroni & Bernardini 2005).

These findings, on the one hand, stress the objective nature of translationese and at the same time underline the unreliability of human assessment. Translationese is not a traditional error insofar as it is not located in a specific part of the text but is manifested cumulatively; it is distributed in the text and is not immediately obvious to the naked eye. The authors present convincing evidence that 'machine learning is reaching a stage in which it is no longer to be considered simply as a cheaper, faster alternative to human labour, but also as a heuristic tool that can help to discover patterns that may not be captured by humans alone' (Baroni & Bernardini 2005: 38). So, it makes sense to work towards employing computer technology in revealing and describing translationese as well as in evaluating target text fluency.

In corpus-based linguistics it is common practice to model language in studied corpora as PoS n-grams. This approach is implemented as part of an experiment to attest specific indicators of simplification and convergence in (Pastor et al. 2008), where shallow-parsed multiple corpora are represented as frequency vectors of PoS 3-grams. Other indicators of similarity in the same research include sentence length in tokens and the type of sentence identified as the number of finite verbs (and their corresponding verbal constructions) in it.

Our previous inquiry into translationese on the same data in (Kutuzov & Kunilovskaya 2015), which was set on lexical level and within a more conventional framework of statistical significance analysis, revealed opposing trends in the frequency of discourse markers - almost the same number of items were significantly overused or underused in translations. These findings can be interpreted in line with the third code hypothesis supported in (Hansen-Schirra 2011). Hansen-Schirra used carefully designed and annotated corpus resources and proved hybrid character of translationese, which manifested opposite tendencies of normalisation and interference for individual register features.

Finally, to the best of our knowledge translated Russian is yet to be investigated in the corpus-based framework, though there has been extensive previous work in the pedagogical and prescriptive area. There is not much research on comparative analysis of Russian corpora either (however, see Mikhailov 2003 where a Russian-Finnish parallel corpus is described, and Kutuzov & Kuzmenko 2015, where machine learning methods are used as well, together with distributional semantics). But we can rule out frequency distribution of PoS n-grams, mentioned in many English-based studies, as a useful indicator of differences between copora due to the fact that word order in Russian is relatively more flexible. It can hardly be used as a crude substitute for syntactic information either, because it does not signal syntactic relations. At the same time it is crucial for structuring information, i.e. for arranging theme and rheme progressions and providing text cohesion (Alekseyenko 2013).

Taking the previous work on corpus-based studies of translated text into consideration, in the next Section we describe our experimental set-up and define the set of linguistic indicators chosen to represent our corpora in the machine learning task.

3 Applying multidimensional analysis to translations

As shown above, our main research question can be formulated as follows: are there any regular differences between translated and non-translated corpora in the typical linguistic environment of sentence boundaries, and which linguistic features (from the set we employ) will the machine learning algorithm mostly draw upon to calculate this difference? In other words, we aim at achieving a twofold objective. First, we want to detect whether a machine is able to learn contrasts between translations and naturally produced texts on the basis of representations of the two corpora built around the lexical and grammatical properties of tokens to the right and to the left of sentence boundary. Second, we want to reveal the indicators that are most informative for this task.

To tackle this, we roughly follow the multidimensional analysis approach established by Gries & Deshors (2014). They explore differences between native speakers and learners or non-native speakers through studying statistical interactions in corpus data. They establish a two-step procedure: a model trained on native data is applied to non-standard texts in order to find cases where their authors made decisions, distinct from what a native speaker would probably do in the same linguistic situation. This approach was successfully applied to a comparison of differences in the usage of *may* and *can* between native English speakers and French and Chinese learners of English.

In the present research, texts translated from English into Russian are considered a kind of a specific Russian language variety that can be compared to a standard or native language. We hypothesize that while translating, native Russians construct sentences differently, and their deviating choices can be revealed through the statistical evaluation of the set of at-the-sentence-boundary-factors offered below. We argue that these features can be used to predict sentence boundaries as a formal structural event indicative of sentence structure. We use data from two corpora:

1. the well-known monolingual Russian National Corpus (further **RNC**) containing non-translated texts by native Russian speakers and extensively described in the literature[1];

2. the parallel Russian Learner Translator Corpus (further **RusLTC**) described in Kutuzov & Kunilovskaya (2014), containing translations from English into Russian and backwards done by Russian translation students from 8 different universities[2]. There are no reference translations in the corpus, but one source can be accompanied by multiple translations.

The RNC represents 'native' Russian language, while the second corpus is arguably a strong case of a non-standard variety ('translationese' in the current research context). From each corpus, we extracted a sub-corpus containing texts belonging to mass-media expository genres, so that the material is as comparable as possible. Overall, our 'standard' corpus consists of 7 679 documents and 8 289 884 word tokens, while translations corpus consists of 1 332 documents and 586 935 word tokens.

In order to evaluate differences between non-translated and translated texts, we employ a number of contextual features in sentence boundaries environments. They were used to train a machine learning model to predict these boundaries. We will now briefly describe the essential details of the process. Our training set (a mass-media sub-corpus of the RNC) lacks manual sentence mark-up. Thus, we first trained a *Punkt* model on the whole RNC (about 150 million tokens). *Punkt* (Kiss & Strunk 2006) is a well-known unsupervised algorithm to learn abbreviations, collocations and typical sentence-starters. After initial training, it

---

[1] See http://ruscorpora.ru/corpora-biblio.html
[2] Available at http://rus-ltc.org

can then be used on raw text to detect sentence boundaries with high accuracy. We applied the trained model to our sub-corpus to split it into sentences. This segmentation is accepted as ground-truth and used further.

We are interested in how various linguistic features correlate with the event of a sentence boundary. Thus, in our approach, word tokens in the text are observed as instances with various linguistic features (attributes). Each instance belongs to exactly one of two classes: either it is the last in the current sentence or not. If it is, it means that its class is 'boundary', otherwise it is a regular token.

Then, the problem is to build a binary classifier which predicts boundary class depending on token features. It is important to note that tokens in our case include punctuation, but not end-of-sentence punctuation marks: those were ignored during training and testing. This is because we are after linguistic features, not trivial orthographic predictors like a full stop or a capitalized word (all tokens were lower-cased). Because of punctuation, the total number of instances in our data sets is slightly higher than stated above: 9,422,955 instances for the RNC corpus and 631,361 instances for the translation corpus.

Initially, we extracted a total of 82 features:

1. current token (instance itself);

2. lemma of the current token[3];

3. part of speech of the current token (one of 19 categories, including punctuation);

4. token length in characters;

5. lemma length in characters (because of rich inflectional system in Russian, it is often quite different from the token length; also, functional words are usually shorter than content ones);

6. accumulated sentence length in tokens (up to the current token);

7. accumulated sentence length in characters;

8. accumulated number of finite verbs in the current sentence;

9. accumulated number of Nominative nouns and pronouns;

---

[3] Lemmatisation and PoS-tagging was performed with the help of state-of-the-art *Mystem* morphological analyser for Russian, described in Segalovich (2003)

10. accumulated number of coordinate conjunctions (including multi-word entities, 26 conjunctions in the list);

11. accumulated number of subordinate conjunctions (including multi-word entities, 56 conjunctions in the list)

12. lemmas of five tokens to the left and five tokens to the right of the current token (further 'neighbours');

13. lengths of lemmas and tokens of the neighbours;

14. binary feature 'is a coordinate conjunction' for all the neighbours;

15. binary feature 'is a subordinate conjunction' for all the neighbours;

16. binary feature 'is a discourse marker' for all the neighbours (discourse markers list comprises 86 elements and includes words like *итак* 'thus', and multi-word entities);

17. part of speech for all the neighbours;

18. binary class attribute (sentence boundary or not), with about 6% of all tokens being boundary.

Not all features possess equal predictive power. First of all, we had to filter out string features (lemmas and tokens themselves). Using text strings as predictors is principally possible, but only with corpora much larger than ours, to overcome the sparsity problem (the majority of words are rare). Also, most classifiers do not work with string attributes: we managed to train Bayes multinomial and stochastic gradient descent models (essentially vectorizing text attributes and then treating them as numerical ones), but performance was much worse than with other features (numerical and categorical/nominal). Thus, we leave this possibility for a future work.

After removing problematic string features, we performed basic feature selection by measuring *information gain* (mutual information, MI) with respect to sentence boundary class for each feature independently in the RNC. Below is a list of the most promising features in descending order, with respective information gain values and identifiers:

1. 0.031049 PoS of the current token (**pos**);

2. 0.022271 PoS of the first token to the right (**pos1R**);

3. 0.010838 length of the current token in characters (**token_length**);

4. 0.010205 length of the current lemma in characters (**lemma_length**);

5. 0.009188 PoS of the first token to the left (**pos1L**);

6. 0.008043 accumulated sentence length in characters (**sent_char_length**);

7. 0.007313 accumulated sentence length in tokens (**sent_length**);

8. 0.005357 accumulated number of finite verbs in the current sentence (**finite_verbs**);

9. 0.005047 PoS of the second token to the right (**pos2R**);

10. 0.004097 is the first token to the right a discourse marker? (**dm1R**);

11. 0.003592 length of the first token to the right (**token_length1R**);

12. 0.002896 is the first token to the right a coordinate conjunction? (**conj1R**);

13. 0.002832 length of the first lemma to the right (**lemma_length1R**);

14. 0.002556 accumulated number of coordinate conjunctions in the current sentence (**conjunctions**);

15. 0.001879 PoS of the third token to the right (**pos3R**).

Additionally, *CfsSubsetEval* the (Correlation-based Feature Subset Selection) algorithm, described in Hall (1998), was used to discover the best subset of features. This information is important, because features may be (and certainly are) interdependent and improve or degrade performance of each other. Bidirectional evaluation of 621 subsets (only globally predictive features[4]) returned the following set of 4 features as the best one:

1. PoS of the current token (**pos**);

2. is the first token to the right a discourse marker? (**dm1R**);

3. is the first token to the right a coordinate conjunction? (**conj1R**);

4. PoS of the first token to the right (**pos1R**).

---

[4] It means that we measured their performance over the whole dataset. This effectively eliminates features which are very predictive at some particular parts of the data (for example, in texts by one author), but useless in the majority of other parts.

Based on this data, we conclude that the best-predicting features are parts of speech for both the current token and its immediate right and left neighbours, length of the current token, the accumulated sentence length in characters and the number of finite verbs. It turns out to be important to look at the functional status of the neighbours: the property of being a discourse marker or a conjunction for the first token to the right ranks high as a predicting feature in our experiments. On the other hand, the features manifesting the length of neighbour tokens do not contribute much to the prediction, but slow down the training. Therefore, these features as well as accumulated number of Nominative nouns and pronouns were filtered out.

The last feature seemed promising initially, but did not provide enough predictive power. We believe the reason is grammatical homonymy: in Russian, Nominative and Accusative forms often coincide for inanimate nouns, and this ambiguity is not resolved by *Mystem*, not without syntactic parsing anyway. We considered a noun to be Nominative only when it was the only possible morphological interpretation, and this is only the case for animate nouns. Thus, in fact this feature reflected the accumulated number of Nominative *animate* nouns. Note that most information potentially delivered by the number of Nominatives is probably already contained in the number of finite verbs (and this feature is closely correlated with boundary class), so, the loss was not big.

The remaining 48 features were used to train a REPTree model (Reduced Error-Pruning Tree, introduced by Quinlan 1987) to predict sentence boundaries in native non-translated mass media texts. Unlike regression used by Gries & Deshors (2014), this algorithm belongs to the family of decision tree learners; we use its implementation in the open-source Weka software package Hall et al. (2009). A decision tree approach was chosen because it allows training on various types of features (predictors): numeric, binary or nominal/categorical. Additionally, decision trees are more human-readable than the output of other machine learning classifiers, though, of course, with large amount of data the model becomes more complex, with tens of thousands branches or more, which makes it not feasible to try to 'read' it directly.

In order to avoid over-fitting and improve accuracy, we used REPTree with the *Bagging* meta-algorithm suggested in Breiman (1996). It essentially multiplies training data through bootstrapping and then trains models on each of resulting sets ('bags'). The predictions from each model are averaged before final output. In our task, it substantially improved performance of the classifier. Thus, we have a model that classifies tokens into boundary (final) and non-boundary ones based on the above mentioned set of features. For each classification (prediction) the model additionally outputs the degree of its confidence in the range {0...1}. We will comment on the performance of this model in Section 4.

Example 1 below illustrates the model's predictions on a piece of Russian text:

(1) ...*но* & *и* & *алмазодобывающим*. & *Сейчас*...
   [non-boundary & non-boundary & boundary & non-boundary]
   ...*but also diamond-producing region. Today*...

The next step is to use this model to 'predict' sentence boundaries in our translation corpus. We expect the model to perform slightly worse, because translations (let alone learners' translations!) are well-known to be linguistically different from non-translations in the same language. The results of testing the previously trained model on translated texts may be used for two purposes: first, to manually inspect cases of the model failing to predict sentence boundaries and possibly gain insights on the reasons, and second, to train another model which predicts not sentence boundaries, but inconsistencies between the first model decisions and what a translator did in a particular context.

In other words, we try to find out which of the above mentioned linguistic features or their combinations are associated with 'non-typical' (or outright erroneous) sentence boundaries in translations. This answers one of the important questions in translation studies (and in cross-linguistic research in general): what patterns of linguistic elements and their characteristics make translations or learner speech in L2 sound non-fluent, foreign and unnatural? Experimental results are described in Section 4.

4 Experimental results

Table 1 shows performance of the first trained model tested on the native corpus (RNC) and on the translation corpus (RusLTC). Overall F_1 (harmonic mean of precision and recall) is a weighted value over both predicted classes, boundary and non-boundary; boundary F_1, precision and recall are the respective values for boundary class only. Performance on detection of the non-boundary tokens is much higher than on the boundary ones, because the first class is much more frequent: it is easier to detect an in-sentence token than a final one. This is the reason behind the difference between overall and boundary performance.

We report precision and recall results, not only purely statistical values like coefficient of determination (R^2) or likelihood ratio. We believe it is more important to evaluate real predictions of the model on the data rather than abstract

Table 1: Performance of sentence boundary detection model

	Overall F_1	Boundary F_1	Boundary precision	Boundary recall
RNC	0.955	0.584	0.873	0.439
RusLTC	0.956	0.522	0.708	0.413

goodness or the regression fit: one is interested in how much noise is present in the model's predictions for each class (precision), and what fraction of instances belonging to this or that class was correctly classified as such. Simply reporting the overall accuracy (percentage of correctly classified instances) is not enough.

Quite often we deal with binary classification tasks, where instances of class A are much rarer than instances of class B. For example, in our data, sentence boundary tokens occur 15 times rarer than the non-boundary ones. The same is true for usage of *can* and *may* in Gries & Deshors (2014): *can* is 2 or 3 times more frequent. In this situation, a classifier can be very reliable for the majority class, but though showing poor quality for the minority class. However, because of larger number of majority class instances, the overall number of correct predictions will be high and accuracy would seem to be quite satisfactory, notwithstanding the fact that the model actually almost never correctly predicts the minority class (and this 'marked' class is often the aim of the whole research). Thus, it is very important to report precision and recall for each class separately, especially for the minority one.

Getting back to our results, we see that despite high overall F_1, the model is not quite perfect in detecting sentence boundaries even in the native corpus it was trained on: more than half of the boundary tokens are not detected as such. However, precision is very high: there is almost no noise in the detected boundary events (Baroni & Bernardini (2005) faced the same situation). It means that not all sentence boundaries correlate well with the features we chose. This is expected and quite natural: Russian sentence structures are highly variable due to relatively flexible word order. Also, sentence boundaries are often influenced by other higher-level linguistic phenomena, such as syntactic dependencies, or semantic and pragmatic structure of the discourse.

However, quite a lot of boundaries are predicted by the formal and morphological characteristics of the elements we employed. As stated earlier, boundary tokens comprise no more than 6% of all instances in the data set (both in native and translated corpora). Consequently, F_1 of the boundary class detection in our model is more than 4 times better than expected $F_1 = 0.1$ of random baseline (choosing one of two classes with equal probability). Thus, our features do provide some signals which are meaningful for predicting sentence boundaries. It means that in non-translated Russian texts there are relatively stable patterns marking such boundaries, which makes it feasible to compare these patterns to ones found in the translation corpus.

It is also encouraging that performance does not drop significantly when the model is applied to the translated corpus: the same regularities generally hold in translated texts as in native ones (they are still in the Russian language, after all). However, both precision and recall are slightly lower, which means that the model makes wrong predictions more often than on the native texts, and thus, the aforementioned patterns of features behave slightly differently in the translated corpus. This also seems quite logical: as stated earlier, translated texts represent a special non-standard variety of Russian, and sequences of items in these texts deviate from the standard ones the model was trained on.

In order to learn which linguistic features from the general list above are associated with these deviations, once again we follow Gries & Deshors (2014)'s approach and compile a dataset with all instances from our translated corpus, their respective features and a new class attribute. This time, instances are divided into two classes, depending on whether the model made a correct or incorrect prediction.

Then, we remove all instances where confidence of the model prediction was below 0.9 to filter out 'weak' decisions[5]. This step leaves us with 548 231 instances, out of 631 thousand total.

For this dataset we perform feature selection as well: from the linguistic point of view, we look for combinations of features that typically accompany non-native behaviour of the text producer. The following features are found to correlate best with the probability of error (the correlation is again calculated as *information gain*):

1. 0.0069041 **pos**;

2. 0.002582 **pos1R**;

3. 0.0025574 **sent_char_length**;

4. 0.0023149 **sent_length**;

5. 0.0022355 **token_length**;

---

[5] Studying weak predictions and correlating them with real translators' decisions also seems promising, but we leave it to future research.

6. 0.0018903 **lemma_length**;

7. 0.0017348 **pos1L**;

8. 0.0014444 **finite_verbs**;

9. 0.0011813 **conjunctions**.

Additionally, the best set of features selected using *CfsSubsetEval* includes **pos, token_length, sent_char_length, finite_verbs, conjunctions, subconj1L, pos1R,** and **subconj2R. dm4R** was selected as a locally predictive feature: it predicts an error only in some contexts, while other features do this globally.

Thus, it is part of speech of the token itself and its immediate neighbour to the right that mostly mark non-native behaviour of learner translators in our RusLTC corpus; accumulated sentence length (it seems that one can safely use either token length or character length) is also among the best predictive features, as well as the length of the current token and, to some extent, the number of conjunctions and finite verbs in the sentence.

Note that if we look at the predictions that the model made in the native texts (RNC corpus) at test time and try to find features correlated with correctness of decisions made, the set of most effective predictors would be different and much weaker. Only one feature (**pos**) achieves the information gain value of 0.002^6, while other features' correlations are an order of magnitude lower and can be considered non-existent. Thus, in native texts, correctness of our model's decisions is not directly dependent on particular features, and its errors are caused by external factors (preprocessing or lemmatising issues, higher linguistic constraints on sentence boundaries, etc). At the same time, in the translation corpus the models' mistakes are often determined by the feature patterns found in the data, rather than by noise or factors outside our reach.

The reference corpus is 15 times larger than the translational one, so it is very unlikely that the model has not seen some patterns of the selected features. We suppose that the model's failure to predict sentence boundaries in translations can be safely attributed to sentence boundary pattern deviations from the standard, found in translations.

Thus, applying the model trained on the comparable reference corpus to the translated texts reveals that they possess intrinsic characteristics different from those of non-translations. Lexical and grammatical features of tokens in the immediate context of sentence boundaries are found to be stably different in cor-

---

[6] Still 3.5 times lower than in the translations.

pora of non-translations and translations. In Section 5 we discuss examples and implications of these findings.

5 Discussion and future work

The analysis of the algorithm's performance on the translation corpus and error modelling led to several interesting insights and observations, described below.

Manual inspection of correlation between instances' parts of speech and the first model errors on the translation corpus indicates that some of PoS yield more errors on the same amount of instances than the others. It means that they are more often included in non-standard sentence boundary patterns in translations. As shown in Figure 1, the parts of speech of the current token that are apt to defy standard Russian regularities include nouns and pronouns in non-nominative cases (**S** and **SPRO**) and tokens for which *Mystem* was not sure about their PoS (**UNKN**). Other parts of speech are more conforming and cause less mistakes, signalling that translators make more natural choices.

Linguistically speaking, it means that there are **contextually identical** situations, in which standard Russian texts usually feature sentence boundary, while translated texts do not (or vice versa). This difference in sentence patterns is most frequently associated with non-nominative nouns and pronouns.

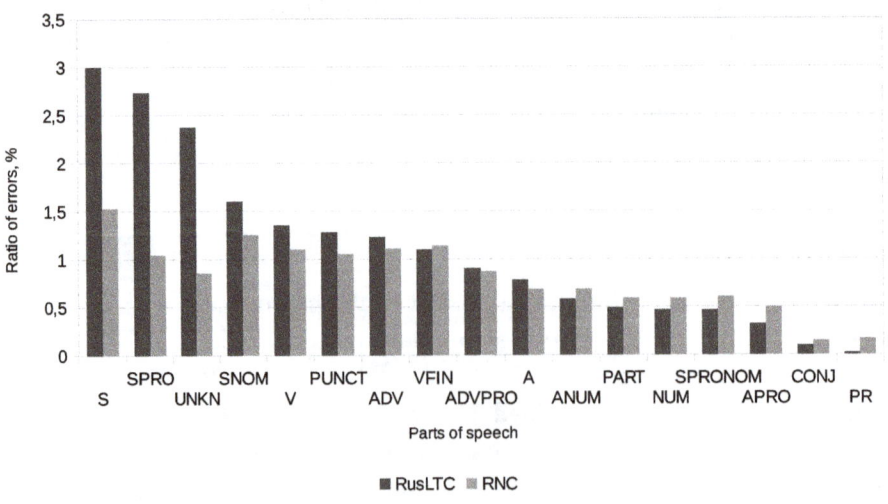

Figure 1: Error rates for PoS values of current token

It is quite logical that the model makes mistakes on 'strange' tokens with unknown PoS (mostly they are foreign words in Latin alphabet, digits or rare abbreviations).

Additionally, such atypical patterns are often caused by interference from English word order. In Example 2 translators routinely reproduce the structure with the final non-nominative pronoun, which is less frequent, but not unacceptable, in non-translated Russian texts (see more detailed explanation below, in the description of **PR_SPRO** pattern).

(2) *Trees rustled above him.*
     Деревья шумели над ним.

Note that the mistakes are rarer on the native texts (see **RNC** bars in Figure 1) for almost all parts of speech where error ratio exceeds 1%, and are on par with the translations in the other cases. Also, non-nominative nouns (S) and pronouns (SPRO) seem to be not so variable as to their positions within a sentence in the reference corpus as in the translation corpus: in the RNC corpus the error ratio for them is almost equal to their nominative counterparts.

As it is clear from the precision/recall metrics and confusion matrix, most model errors occur when the model does not predict an actual sentence boundary in the translated texts (false negatives). Sentence boundaries predicted in the middle of running sentences (false positives) are far less frequent errors: they account for only 5% of all model failures. It means that the model does cover some real contextual patterns where sentence boundaries are typical for RNC, but it does not observe these patterns in translated data, given our feature set. For the purposes of this exploratory work we decided to prefer precision to recall and did not try to cover other (numerous) cases, when sentence boundaries are not described by our features.

Figure 2 illustrates this with the **pos1R** feature (PoS of the first token to the right of the current one). Bottom parts of the chart bars represent cases where the actual SB was missed by the model, because the observed sequence of linguistic features is problematic for the model trained on the standard language variety (false negatives), while the top ones represent cases where SB was predicted after tokens that actually were not final in translations (unlikely non-boundary tokens, false positives).

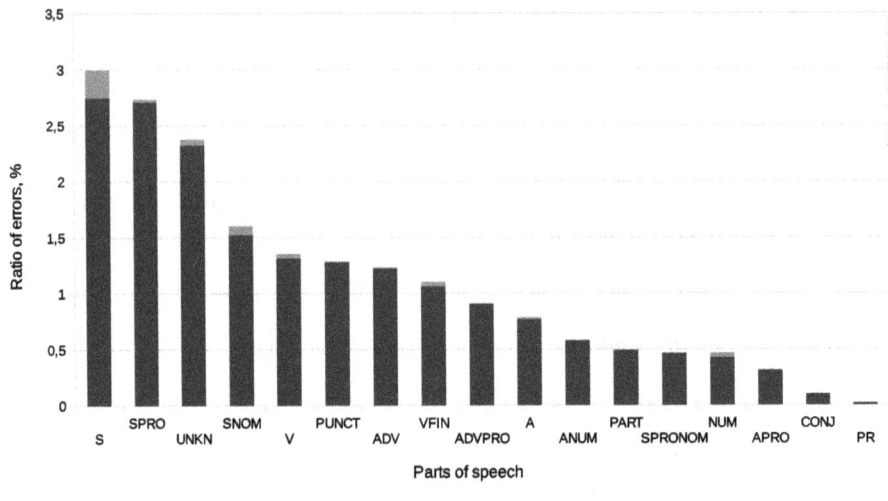

Figure 2: Error rates for PoS values of the first token to the right; evaluation on translational data

Interestingly, the ratio of false positives for some PoS of the nearest neighbour to the right is unusually high (higher than 5% of all errors, which is the mean value over the whole corpus): precisely, for **S** and **NUM**, and to some extent for **SNOM**. Thus, translators comparatively more often continue sentences with numeral words (including lexical units like *оба* 'both' or *полтора* 'one and a half'), while in the same situation in the native texts we would expect the sentence to end, and a new sentence to start with this numeral.

Similar observation can be made concerning particular binary features, which also seem predictive of non-standard translators' behaviour. For example, the probability of an error is almost two times higher (2% probability) when the next token to the right belongs to the set of discourse markers (like *в сущности* 'in fact', *наверное* 'perhaps'), manifested in the feature **dm1R**. These errors are distributed almost evenly between false negatives (69%) and false positives (31%), leading to a false positives ratio that is 6 times higher than the average over the corpus. This is because under the same circumstances in standard Russian the sentence would end, and the new sentence would be started with a discourse marker, but translators decide to continue the sentence, joining it with the next. Thus, the model yields a false positive in detecting a sentence boundary token immediately to the left of the marker. Note that when the **dm1R** feature takes the 'False' value (the first-to-the-right token is not a discourse marker) the distribution of false negatives and false positives is quite standard: 95% vs 5%.

Despite the fact that RusLTC contains more sentences starting with one of the discourse markers from our list (7,28% of all sentences) than RNC (5,66%, the difference is statistically significant), it also contains sentences with atypical in-sentence position of typical sentence-initials. Thus, our strategy of revealing translationese overcomes limitations of the traditional statistical significance analysis.

Consider the translation in Example 3 to the English source text:

(3) *The findings have broken down some of the illusions commonly associated with burglaries; with four out of five revealing burglary was not opportunistic,* **instead** *returning to a property a number of times before breaking in (Daily Mail, Nov. 1, 2011).*
Результаты исследования разрушили некоторые мифы, касающиеся краж со взломом, **так** *например, четыре из пяти раскрытых преступлений не были незапланированными,* **напротив***, грабители несколько раз возвращались на место потенциального взлома прежде, чем вторгнуться в чужой дом.*

The information units after the English semi-colon and after 'instead' are both rendered as well-formed separate discourse units, each with their own discourse markers, but these potential sentences are unreasonably jammed into one formal structure.

The difference is even more striking with the feature **subconj1R** (whether the next token is a subordinate conjunction or its equivalent). When this feature takes the 'True' value, the ratio of false positives is close to 50%. It means that the model expects to observe more sentences that start with a subordinate conjunction (e.g., *затем* 'then' or *если* 'if') than is the case with the learner translations. It seems to speak in favour of the normalisation hypothesis in translation. Traditional stylistics frowns upon starting a sentence with a subordinate conjunction and translators are opposed to using these less standard opportunities of the language system, which leads to a flatter, less varied expression typical for translations and to lower frequencies of more peripheral elements in them.

Note that our specific interest to false positives is also rooted in the expectations from our previous research Kutuzov & Kunilovskaya (2015), which showed that sentence length in translations is significantly higher than in non-translated texts (from the same sub-corpora). Our belief was that an algorithm like the one reported here should return more false positives for longer sentences, especially as sentence length is among the best predictors in both models. The experiment indeed shows that there is a strong (0.72) exponential correlation between sentence length in characters and the number of false positives; for false negatives this correlation is even higher and reaches the value of 0.8. Thus, statistical modelling approach seems to support the observation that (learner) translations tend to over-use long sentences and this leads to a 'foreign' flavour of the produced texts. In the future, we plan to conduct a more thorough investigation into how and why error rate increases in correlation with sentence length.

Such analysis can be easily made more granular and multi-factorial: we can test for correlation between *sets* of features and non-standard language usage. For example, after ranking patterns **pos+pos1R** by the probability of false negatives, the sequence **SPRO+CONJ** (non-nominative pronoun followed by conjunction) is found on top of the list, with the model failing to predict sentence boundary in almost 10% of its occurrences. Examples of such contexts include sequences like '*которые попадаются у него на пути или похожи на* **них**. *И такие поступки бросают...*'[7] (boundary token is given in bold). It seems that when preceded by a non-nominative pronoun, such a sentence start is rather unnatural: if the first sentence instead ends in a nominative pronoun, the model makes mistakes in less than 2% of such cases. As expected, there are no false positives for both of these patterns.

Another interesting pattern is **pos1L+pos**. The top of the list is dominated by patterns like **V_SPRONOM, VFIN_SPRO, V_SPRO** (pronouns preceded by verbs) and **PR_SPRO** (pronouns preceded by prepositions). 5-6 % of all their instances produce false negative results. This can be explained by English-based interference: typical English sentences ending in non-rhematic (prepositional) phrases get diligently copied into Russian translations. See the following examples 4 - 7 of sentence ends:

(4) ...*until you can clearly define and understand what is being conveyed you cannot hope* **to translate it**.
...*пока вы не можете ясно определить и понять то, что имеется в виду, не надейтесь* **перевести это**. (V_SPRONOM)

(5) ...*with which he* **identified himself**.
..*с которыми он* **ассоциировал себя**. (VFIN_SPRO)

---

[7] ...which are on his way or similar to **them**. And such actions make...

(6) ...*even sometimes obliging a Great Power to tail along **after him**.*
...*иногда даже заставляющим великие державы* **подчиняться ему**.
(V_SPRO)

(7) *It was the end of books **for me**.*
*Книги перестали существовать **для меня**.* (PR_SPRO)

In all these cases putting the rhematic verb in the end of the sentence, after the pronoun, would sound much more natural and close to a native text. Such cases of translationese are detected by our approach: the model trained on the native corpus 'stumbles' at these sequences and rejects to acknowledge that this is the end of the sentence. Thus, this is another example of morphosyntactic feature sets that are perceived by a native speaker as somewhat unnatural, and that are computationally detectable in our approach.

There is one **pos+pos1R** pattern in which the ratio of false positives exceeds the average over the corpus, comprising more than 6% of all errors. It is **S+ADVPRO** (non-nominative noun followed by an adverbial pronoun). False positives in this pattern are often due to translators' punctuation errors. For example, in the fragment '*морского побережья, открытых земель, мест обитания и* **мест** *куда художники и обычные люди могли бы*'[8] it would be correct in Russian to insert a comma after '*мест*'. Without it the model supposes a sentence boundary (perhaps, the lack of finite verbs in this sentence is another reason for the wrong prediction).

We have also detected the tendency for learner translators to overuse pronouns, such as *это* 'this, it' and *здесь* 'here', *так* 'so' at the end of the sentence, which can be the English source text 'shining through'.

Given above are only some examples of 'translationese' discovered by our approach; in fact, this list can be continued and expanded. It is, however, already clear that a researcher can draw numerous insights analysing the output of an algorithm modelling 'native speaker' (in our case, an author of a non-translated text) applied to translations. For example, one can find translations which are most different from native text by simply calculating the density of model mistakes in the given documents. Interestingly, in our material, such procedure revealed several student translations which, upon manual inspection, were obviously produced by machine translation (students cheated).

We emphasize that these differences in the structure of native and translated texts are not always the sign of 'lower quality' of the latter. Differences can be caused by one of translation universals (see example with normalization above)

---

[8] ...of seaside, open lands, habitats and **places** where artists and common people could...

and do not necessarily negatively impact the language of translation. However, detecting 'syntactic translationese' can still be helpful in many settings.

At the same time, manual error analysis brought to our attention several issues with the model design to be addressed in future work. First of all, the model does not distinguish between different punctuation signs, and fails to recognize sentence boundaries before inverted commas opening a sentence; a lot of mistakes come from inverted commas used to set off trademarks, titles and some proper names.

Much noise comes from the binary features that involved multiword discourse markers, which were considered as one lexical unit. The latter proved to be sometimes homonymous to nominal phrases with preposition, and this led to unreasonable predictions. To be a truly reliable feature, these elements need to be disambiguated. Also, some normalization for numbers is needed: as of now, all numbers written in figures are referred to unknown category, which makes a good deal of instances less usable.

We believe that the model would benefit from adding at least several lexical features as strings. As stated above, for now we excluded all string features because of computational complexity and their high dependency on semantics of the utterance. However, a number of words typically accompanying sentence boundaries can be selected and employed.

Thus, our future work in this area should include attempts to decrease the noise in the output through more thoughtful formatting and add new and better-motivated features to the corpora representation, including syntactic ones.

6 Conclusion

The work described above is an attempt to apply multi-factorial statistical analysis to study a variant of the Russian language instantiated in learner translations. We trained machine learning models that detect cases of dissonance between translated and non-translated texts based on a set of formal and morphological features and sentence properties. The approach is tested on traditional for this task monolingual corpora (the reference corpus of non-translated Russian texts and a corpus of comparable learner translations from English into Russian).

Differences between translated and non-translated texts are detected with reference to sentence boundaries, an important structural event, which serves here as a comparability factor. We hypothesize that sentence boundaries in the two corpora are dissimilar in terms of their morphosyntactic environments, and support this claim with empirical evidence.

We analysed variation in sentence patterns between learner-translated and non-translated Russian mass-media texts on the basis of surface and morpho-syntactic parameters of sentence boundaries context. We employed a sliding window of 10 tokens (5 to the left and 5 to the right of a possible sentence boundary) and their associated features to train a classifier which tries to predict whether the current token is the end of the sentence or not. The trained model was then applied to translated texts to find out differences in typical sentence boundaries patterns.

In our experiments, the model trained on the native texts served as a 'mechanical intelligence' representing an average native speaker of Russian making decisions about whether the sentence is going to end in this particular position or not. Comparing this models' decisions with real sentence boundaries in the translated texts allowed to automatically reveal several repeating patterns of features, frequently pointing at cases of 'translationese' typical for learner translators. Thus, this two-step methodology proved fruitful for our aims.

In the future we plan to enrich it with higher-level indicators, such as syntactic dependencies, anaphoric and co-referential chains, semantic data or, maybe, discourse relations, to build up knowledge about sentence boundary as a discourse structural event. Meanwhile, our approach makes it possible to detect sentence boundaries atypical for native texts. This is another step towards an automatic translationese spotter, widely sought in the field of computational translation studies.

7 Acknowledgements

This work has been partly supported by the Russian Foundation for Basic Research within Project No. 17-06-00107. The authors thank the anonymous reviewers for their helpful comments, which were crucial in guiding our work into the right direction. However, all mistakes and inconsistencies remain the responsibility of the authors alone.

References

Alekseyenko, Nataliya V. 2013. *A corpus-based study of theme and thematic progression in English and Russian non-translated texts and in Russian translated texts*. Kent State University PhD thesis.

Baker, Mona. 2004. A corpus-based view of similarity and difference in translation. *International Journal of Corpus Linguistics* 9(2). 167–193.

Baker, Mona. 2011. *In other words: A coursebook on translation*. Amsterdam/Philadelphia: Routledge.

Baroni, Marco & Silvia Bernardini. 2005. A new approach to the study of translationese: Machine-learning the difference between original and translated text. *Literary and Linguistic Computing* 21(3). 259–274.

Bernardini, Silvia. 2007. Collocations in translated language: Combining parallel, comparable and reference corpora. In *Fourth Corpus Linguistics Conference held at the University of Birmingham*, 27–30.

Blum-Kulka, Shoshana. 1986. Shifts of cohesion and coherence in translation. *Interlingual and intercultural communication: Discourse and cognition in translation and second language acquisition studies*.

Breiman, Leo. 1996. Bagging predictors. *Machine Learning* 24(2). 123–140.

Carston, Robyn & Bergljot Behrens. 2007. Making connections–linguistic or pragmatic? In Randi Alice Nilsen, Nana Aba Appiah Amfo & Kaja Borthen (eds.), *Interpreting utterances: Pragmatics and its interfaces*, 51–78. Oslo: Novus Press.

Castagnoli, Sara. 2011. Exploring variation and regularities in translation with multiple translation corpora. *Rassegna Italiana di Linguistica Applicata* 43(1). 311–332.

Chesterman, Andrew. 2010. Why study translation universals? In R. Hartama-Heinonen Kiasm & P. Kukkonen (eds.), *Acta translatologica helsingiensia*, 38–48. Helsinki: Helsingin yliopisto, Suomen kielen, suomalais-ugrilaisten ja pohjoismaisten kielten ja kirjallisuuksien laitos.

Dai, Guangrong & Richard Xiao. 2011. "SL shining through" in translational language: A corpus-based study of Chinese translation of English passives. *Translation Quarterly* 62. 85–108.

Fabricius-Hansen, Cathrine. 1999. Information packaging and translation: Aspects of translational sentence splitting (German–English/Norwegian). *Studia Grammatica* 47. 175–214.

Gile, Daniel. 2008. Local cognitive load in simultaneous interpreting and its implications for empirical research. *Forum* 6(2). 59–77.

Granger, Sylviane. 2010. Comparable and translation corpora in cross-linguistic research: Design, analysis and applications. *Journal of Shanghai Jiaotong University* 2. 14–21.

Grenoble, Lenore A. 1998. *Deixis and information packaging in Russian discourse* (Pragmatics & Beyond New Series 50). Amsterdam & Philadelphia: John Benjamins Publishing.

Gries, Stefan Th. & Sandra C. Deshors. 2014. Using regressions to explore deviations between corpus data and a standard target: Two suggestions. *Corpora* 9(1). 109–136.

Guzmán, Alexandria E. & Celia M. Klin. 2000. Maintaining global coherence in reading: The role of sentence boundaries. *Memory & Cognition* 28(5). 722–730.

Hall, Mark. 1998. *Correlation-based feature subset selection for machine learning*. Hamilton, New Zealand: University of Waikato PhD thesis.

Hall, Mark, Eibe Frank, Geoffrey Holmes, Bernhard Pfahringer, Peter Reutemann & Ian H. Witten. 2009. The WEKA data mining software: An update. *SIGKDD Explorer Newsletter* 11(1). 10–18. DOI:10.1145/1656274.1656278

Hansen-Schirra, Silvia. 2011. Between normalization and shining-through: Specific properties of English-German translations and their influence on the target language. *Multilingual Discourse Production: Diachronic and Synchronic Perspectives* 12. 133–162.

Hatim, Basil & Ian Mason. 1990. *Discourse and the translator*. London & New York: Longman.

Hatim, Basil & Ian Mason. 2005. *The translator as communicator*. London/New York: Routledge.

Hinkel, Eli. 2001. Matters of cohesion in L2 academic texts. *Applied Language Learning* 12(2). 111–132.

Kachroo, Balkrishan. 1984. Textual cohesion and translation. *Méta: Journal des traducteurs* 29(2). 128–134.

Kiss, Tibor & Jan Strunk. 2006. Unsupervised multilingual sentence boundary detection. *Computational Linguistics* 32(4). 485–525.

Koppel, Moshe, Shlomo Argamon & Anat Rachel Shimoni. 2002. Automatically categorizing written texts by author gender. *Literary and Linguistic Computing* 17(4). 401–412.

Kutuzov, Andrey & Maria Kunilovskaya. 2014. Russian learner translator corpus. In Petr Sojka, Aleš Horák, Ivan Kopeček & Karel Pala (eds.), *Text, speech and dialogue* (Lecture Notes in Computer Science 8655 8655), 315–323. Springer International Publishing. DOI:10.1007/978-3-319-10816-2_39

Kutuzov, Andrey & Maria Kunilovskaya. 2015. A quantitative study of translational Russian (based on a translational learner corpus). In *Proceedings of Corpus Linguistics 2015 Conference*, 33–40. Saint Petersburg State University.

Kutuzov, Andrey & Elizaveta Kuzmenko. 2015. Comparing neural lexical models of a classic national corpus and a web corpus: The case for Russian. In Alexander Gelbukh (ed.), *Computational linguistics and intelligent text process-

ing (Lecture Notes in Computer Science 9041), 47–58. Springer International Publishing. DOI:10.1007/978-3-319-18111-0_4

Laviosa, Sara. 1998. Core patterns of lexical use in a comparable corpus of English narrative prose. *Meta: Journal des traducteursMeta:/Translators' Journal* 43(4). 557–570.

Meyer, Thomas & Andrei Popescu-Belis. 2012. Using sense-labeled discourse connectives for statistical machine translation. In *Proceedings of the Joint Workshop on Exploiting Synergies between Information Retrieval and Machine Translation (ESIRMT) and Hybrid Approaches to Machine Translation (HyTra)*, 129–138. Association for Computational Linguistics.

Mikhailov, Mikhail. 2003. *Parallel'nye korpusa xudo estvennyx tekstov: Principy sostavlenija i vozmožnosti primenenija v lingvističeskix i perevodovedcheskix issledovanijax*. University of Tampere PhD thesis.

Olohan, Maeve. 2001. Spelling out the optionals in translation: A corpus study. *UCREL Technical Papers* 13. 423–432.

Pastor, G. Corpas, Ruslan Mitkov, Naveed Afzal & Viktor Pekar. 2008. Translation universals: Do they exist? A corpus-based NLP study of convergence and simplification. In *8th AMTA conference*, 75–81.

Quinlan, J. Ross. 1987. Simplifying decision trees. *International journal of man-machine studies* 27(3). 221–234.

Ramm, Wiebke. 2006. Dispensing with subordination in Translation-Consequences on discourse structure. In Torgrim Solstad, Atle Grønn & Dag Haug (eds.), *A festschrift for Kjell Johan Sæbø*, 121–136. Oslo: University of Oslo.

Rayson, Paul, Xiaolan Xu, Jian Xiao, Anthony Wong & Qi Yuan. 2008. Quantitative analysis of translation revision: Contrastive corpus research on native English and Chinese translationese. In *XVIII fit world congress*.

Segalovich, Ilya. 2003. A fast morphological algorithm with unknown word guessing induced by a dictionary for a web search engine. In *MLMTA*, 273–280.

Solfjeld, Kåre. 2008. Sentence splitting and discourse structure in translations. *Languages in Contrast* 8(1). 21–46.

Štěpánek, Jan & Petr Pajas. 2010. Querying diverse treebanks in a uniform way. *International Journal of Learner Corpus Research* 1(1). 1828–1835.

Unger, Christoph. 2011. Exploring the borderline between procedural encoding and pragmatic inference. In, vol. 25, 103. Leiden: Brill.

van Dijk, Teun A. 1976. Philosophy of action and theory of narrative. *Poetics* 5(4). 287–338.

van Halteren, Hans. 2007. Author verification by linguistic profiling: An exploration of the parameter space. *ACM Transactions on Speech and Language Processing (TSLP)* 4(1). 1.

Xiao, Richard, Lianzhen He & Ming Yue. 2010. In pursuit of the third code: Using the ZJU corpus of translational Chinese in translation studies. In Richard Xiao (ed.), *Using corpora in contrastive and translation studies*, 182–214. Cambridge: Cambridge Scholars Publishing.

Zanettin, Federico. 2013. Corpus methods for descriptive translation studies. *Procedia-Social and Behavioral Sciences* 95. 20–32.

Chapter 6

Cohesion and translation variation: Corpus-based analysis of translation varieties

Ekaterina Lapshinova-Koltunski

Saarland University

> In this study, we analyse cohesion in human and machine translations that we call 'translation varieties' as defined by Lapshinova-Koltunski (2017) – translation types differing in the translation methods involved. We expect variation in the distribution of different cohesive devices which occur in translations. Variation in translation can be caused by different factors, e.g. by systemic contrasts or ambiguities in both source and target languages. It is known that variation in English-to-German translations depends on devices of cohesion involved. We extract quantitative evidence for cohesive devices from a corpus and analyse them with descriptive techniques to see where the differences lie. We include not only English-German translation into our analyses, but also also English and German non-translated texts, representing the source and the target language. Similarities and differences between translated and non-translated texts could provide us with the information on the original of this variation, which might be caused by translationese features.

1 Introduction

This contribution is aimed at the analysis of cohesion in multilingual texts, focussing on variation of cohesive features influenced by different dimensions, i.e. text production type (original vs. translation), translation method involved (manual vs. automatic), as well as systemic contrasts between source and target languages. We know from various studies that translations differ from originals, if various linguistic properties are taken into account (Baker 1995; Teich 2003;

Ekaterina Lapshinova-Koltunski. 2017. Cohesion and translation variation: Corpus-based analysis of translation varieties. In Katrin Menzel, Ekaterina Lapshinova-Koltunski & Kerstin Kunz (eds.), *New perspectives on cohesion and coherence*, 95–118. Berlin: Language Science Press. DOI:10.5281/zenodo.814468

Hansen-Schirra, Neumann & Steiner 2012: and others). These properties of translations distinguishing them from non-translated texts are called *translationese*[1]. In our own studies, i.e. Lapshinova-Koltunski (2015b) and Lapshinova-Koltunski (2015a), we have shown that translations, regardless of the method they were produced with, are different from their source texts and from the comparable originals in the target language. In the latter work (Lapshinova-Koltunski 2015a), we used a set of cohesive features and explorative statistical techniques (automatic classification and correspondence analysis) to discover these differences. In this work, we are using the same set of features, applying descriptive methods which are appropriate for a detailed analysis, zooming into concrete features, such as reference, conjunctive relations and general nouns, as well as their subtypes. This method is supposed to help us to directly compare the differences that we discovered in our previous analyses, and to possibly find out the reasons for the observed variation. Thus, we explicitly compare the feature values and their frequency changes in German and English non-translated texts, as well as human and machine translations from English into German.

Our previous results have also shown that we are not able to discover considerable differences between human and machine translation (MT) in terms of cohesive features if we look at the entire set of features at once. However, we are not convinced that the quality of machine-translated texts can be comparable to that of human-translated ones. For instance, as shown in the examples (1), (2) and (3) ((2) was translated with *Google translate* and (3) was translated by a human), ambiguities cannot be resolved. And in general, translation of coreference and other cohesive devices is poor.

(1) *Alte Mönchsregel: Wenn deine Augen eine Frau erblicken, schlage sie nieder.*

(2) *Ancient monastic rule: When your eyes behold a woman, beat <u>her</u> down.*

(3) *Ancient monastic rule: When your eyes behold a woman, cast <u>them</u> down.*

Although considerable research aimed at enhancing machine-translated texts with textual properties achieved positive results in the recent years, see Webber et al. (2013), Hardmeier (2014) or Meyer, Hajlaoui & Popescu-Belis (2015), document-wide properties of automatically translated texts in terms of coherence still require improvement, as translation models are induced from stand-alone pairs of sentences. Moreover, target language models approximate the

---

[1] The term was invoked by Gellerstam (1986).

target language on the string level only, whereas target texts have properties that go beyond those of their individual sentences and that reveal themselves in the frequency and distribution of more abstract categories. Here we mean a certain type of a pronoun or its function instead of the pronoun itself. A more abstract category of the pronouns *he* and *his* would be PERSONAL HEAD or PERSONAL MODIFIER, and for the pronoun *this* – DEMONSTRATIVE HEAD or DEMONSTRATIVE MODIFIER, depending on the context of its occurrence.

We apply corpus-based methods to analyse frequencies and distributions of such cohesive categories in a multilingual corpus that contains English and German originals, as well as multiple translations into German produced with several methods, including manual and automatic ones. Frequencies of cohesive devices will be automatically extracted from the corpus on the basis of automatic pre-processing with a part-of-speech tagger. We are aware of possible errors caused by erroneous tagger output. However, the decision for automatic identification of categories is justified by the fact that we would like to use the knowledge for machine translation, which requires categories that can be annotated automatically with reasonable accuracy. So, we rely on the accuracies of the state-of-the-art tools at hand. The distributions of these categories will then be analysed in originals and translations, as well as in human and machine translations. We will also pay attention to differences between original English and German, as they will serve as a kind of baseline for identifying SHINING THROUGH and NORMALISATION – translationese features resulting from the language contrast between source and target languages.

The obtained information on the differences will be valuable for translation and language contrast studies, and may also find application in multilingual natural language processing (NLP), especially in MT.

2 Theoretical issues and related work

2.1 Cohesion and cohesive devices

COHESION refers to the text-internal relationship of linguistic elements that are overtly linked via lexico-grammatical devices across sentences to be understood as a text, and occurs where the interpretation of some element in the text is dependent on that of another (Halliday & Hasan 1976). Cohesion is related to coherence, whose recognition in a text is more subjective. It involves text- and reader-based features, and refers to illocutionary relations within a discourse. Coherence is the logical flow of interrelated ideas in a text. According to Halliday & Hasan (1976), what distinguishes cohesive relations from other semantic relations is that the lexico-grammatical resources trigger relations that transcend the boundaries of the clause.

The lexico-grammatical devices linking elements in a text and triggering semantic relationships are called COHESIVE DEVICES. They include personal and demonstrative pronouns and modifiers, substitute forms, elliptical constructions and conjunctions, or lexical devices such as nouns, adjectives and verbs. We will concentrate on two main types of devices: coreference and conjunction, which represent explicit linguistic devices signalling particular conceptual relations to linguistic elements in other text parts (see Halliday & Hasan 1976; Halliday & Matthiessen 2013). These devices are grammar-driven, as most of their items belong to a closed class of functional items.

Coreference and conjunction differ in the conceptual relations that they trigger. Whereas coreference expresses identity to a referent mentioned in another textual part, conjunctions indicate logico-semantic relations between referents, and do not have antecedents, as they do not refer themselves (see Lapshinova-Koltunski & Kunz 2014; Kunz & Lapshinova-Koltunski 2015).

Halliday & Hasan (1976) distinguish three types of coreference: PERSONAL, expressed with personal pronouns, possessives and modifiers, as in example (4), DEMONSTRATIVE, expressed by demonstrative pronouns, definite articles, local and temporal adverbs, as well as pronominal adverbs, see example (5), and COMPARATIVE, expressed by adjectives and adverbs of comparison, as in (6).

(4) *Young men on the roof tops changed their tune; spit and fiddled with the mouthpiece for a while and when [they] put it back in and blew out their cheeks it was just like the light of that day, pure and steady and kind of kind.*

(5) *But no woman ever tried to humiliate him before, to his knowledge, and Fevvers has both tried and succeeded. [This] has set up a conflict between his own hitherto impregnable sense of self-esteem and the lack of esteem with which the woman treats him.*

(6) *Sandy beaches, water sports and activities, evening entertainment and a variety of restaurants make this an ideal base for an active holiday. For a [quieter] and [more relaxing] time or perhaps a walking holiday, go further west...*

As the category of comparative reference is semantically distinct from the first two types (it evokes the relation of similarity or comparison, and not identity, cf.

Halliday & Matthiessen (2004)), we will exclude it from our analysis. Yet, we include another device related to coreference – GENERAL NOUNS. This category is mostly referred to as lexical cohesion, as general nouns are lexical items. However, most of them are cases of abstract anaphora (see Zinsmeister, Dipper & Seiss 2012), or extended reference, and should be, therefore, classified as coreference. In example (7), *this assumption* does not refer to a nominal phrase, but to a clause in the previous sentence. This noun conceptually outlines complex pieces of information, and could also be replaced by the demonstrative pronoun *this*.

(7) It is only logical to think that *if some choice is good, more is better; people who care about having infinite options will benefit from them, and those who do not always just ignore the 273 versions of cereal they have never tried*. Yet recent research strongly suggests that, psychologically, [this assumption] is wrong.

Following Halliday & Hasan (1976), we also distinguish five categories of conjunctive devices classified according to the semantic relations they convey: 1) additive – relation of addition, e.g. *and, in addition, furthermore*; 2) adversative – relation of contrast/alternative, such as *but, by contrast, though*; 3) causal – relation of causality or dependence, such as *because, that is why, therefore*; 4) temporal – temporal relation (*afterwards, at the same time*); and 5) modal – interpersonal and pragmatic relation (*unfortunately, surely, of course*). Most grammars do not include devices of the latter category, which is, however, an important component of a meaningful discourse, as events are connected by speaker's evaluation. Halliday & Hasan (1976) call them 'continuatives'.

2.2 Cohesion in contrastive studies and translation

Cohesion and coherence have been analysed in a number of works on language contrasts dealing with English and German, in which corpus-based methods have become increasingly popular in recent years. However, most multilingual studies are still concerned with individual cohesive devices in particular registers, see Bührig & House (2004) for selected cohesive conjunctions or adverbs in prepared speeches, Zinsmeister, Dipper & Seiss (2012) for abstract anaphora in parliament debates, and Taboada & Gómez-González (2012) for particular coherence relations in a number of different registers. The latter, however, considers also variation in spoken and written language. The authors state that the differences between spoken and written dimensions are more prominent than between languages. Kunz & Lapshinova-Koltunski (2015) and Kunz et al. (2017) also show discrepancy between spoken and written texts, and demonstrate that the distributions of different cohesive devices are register-dependent. The authors show this for a number of cohesive phenomena, analysing structural and functional subtypes of coreference, substitution, discourse connectives, and ellipsis. Their dataset includes several registers, and they are able to identify contrasts and commonalities across languages and registers with respect to the subtypes of all cohesive devices under analysis, showing that these languages differ in the degree of variation between individual registers. Moreover, there is more variation in the realisation of cohesive devices in German than in English. The authors attested the main differences in terms of preferred meaning relations: a preference for explicitly realising logico-semantic relations by conjunctions and a tendency to realise relations of identity by coreference. Interestingly, similar meaning relations are realised by different subtypes of discourse phenomena in different languages and registers.

Cross-lingual contrasts stated on the basis of non-translated data are also of great importance for translation. Kunz et al. (2017) suggest preferred translation strategies on the basis of contrastive interpretations for the results of their quantitative analysis, which show that language contrasts are even more pronounced if we compare languages within each register. These contrasts exist in the features used for creating cohesive relations. Therefore, they suggest that, when translating popular science texts from English into German, translators should use linguistic means expressing cohesive relations more extensively. Overall, they claim that translators should use more explicit devices translating from English into German. For instance, demonstrative pronouns should be used more often instead of personal pronouns: *dies/das* ("this") instead of *es* ("it"). The opposite translation strategies are used when translating from German to English. However, studies of translated language show that translators do not necessarily apply such strategies. Zinsmeister, Dipper & Seiss (2012) demonstrate that translations in general tend to preserve the categories, functions and positions of the source language anaphoras, which results in SHINING THROUGH of the source language preferences (Teich 2003) – in both translation directions. Additionally, due to the tendency to explicate textual relations, translators tend to use more nominal coreference instead of pronominal coreference. EXPLICITATION – the tendency of translations to be more explicit than their sources (Vinay & Darbelnet 1958; Blum-Kulka 1986) – along with *shining through*, belong to the characteristics of translated texts caused by peculiarities of translation process. This translation property forms the focus of studies on the usage of discourse connectives in both manual and automatic translation (see Becher 2011; Bisiada 2014; Meyer & Webber 2013; Li, Carpuat & Nenkova 2014b). Becher (2011) analyses additions (explicitation) and omissions (IMPLICITATION) of conjunctive adverbials in business texts, focussing on both English-to-German and German-to-English translations. The author observes more explicitation in the translation direction English-to-German than in the other direction. On the one hand, this is caused by the fact that German has a richer inventory of linguistic triggers for this type of relations (see Becher 2011; Kunz & Lapshinova-Koltunski 2014). But on the other, this is also due to translation properties: they tend towards splitting up information that is presented in one sentence in the source text into two sentences in the target text. This was confirmed by a number of studies (such as Fabricius-Hansen 1999; Doherty 2004; Bisiada 2014). The latter demonstrates that sentence-splitting is a frequent strategy when translating from English into German.

We show that both human and machine translations from English into German differ from their source texts, and also from the comparable German originals, if cohesion and other discourse features are considered (Lapshinova-Koltunski 2015a). This coincides with one of the features defined within the studies of translationese (see Gellerstam 1986; Baker 1993). According to these studies, translations have their own specific features distinguishing them from the source texts and comparable originals in the target language. One of the features distinguishing them from non-translated texts is LEVELLING OUT or CONVERGENCE (Laviosa-Braithwaite 2002) – individual translated texts are more alike than individual non-translated texts. According to Laviosa-Braithwaite (2002), this implies a relatively higher level of homogeneity of translated texts with regard to their own scores in contrast to originals, which would also mean that variation across these texts should be lower than across non-translated ones. As already mentioned above, we believe that translation features are partly effected by the source or the target language involved. Shining through, which was mentioned earlier in this section, is one of these features, and means that we can observe certain features of the source texts in translations. At the same time, we can have an opposite effect, called (over-)NORMALISATION – a tendency to exaggerate features of the target language and to conform to its typical patterns.

2.3 Cohesion in human and machine translations

Differences between human and machine translation in terms of cohesive features have been demonstrated in a number of studies that try to incorporate cohesion-related properties into MT, or use them for MT evaluation.

Li, Carpuat & Nenkova (2014a) show in their experiments that discourse usage may affect machine translation between some language pairs for particular logico-semantic relations. Mascarell et al. (2014) compare translations of German nominal compounds into English, presenting a system that helps to consistently translate coreference via compounds. Guillou (2013) compares lexical consistency (as a part of lexical cohesion) in human and machine translation. Meyer & Webber (2013) analyse explicitation and implicitation of discourse connectives in translation, comparing the occurrence of these phenomena in human and machine translations. Hardmeier (2012), Guillou (2012) and Hardmeier (2014) analyse translation of pronominal anaphora in statistical machine translation, trying to improve performance of their systems.

Most of these studies use human translations as references for evaluating machine ones, whereas direct comparison is carried out in a few cases only. In our own study (Lapshinova-Koltunski 2015a), we compare human and machine translations with each other, and also with comparable source and target texts, analysing a set of cohesive features and their distributions across texts. However, we were not able to show where the differences between human- and machine-translated texts lie, as the observed variation seemed to be more influenced by register than by translation method.

Therefore, in this study, we do not pay attention to the registers that a given text belongs to, and analyse translations applying univariate techniques, assuming that this would allow us to directly observe differences between not only translated and non-translated texts, but also between manual and automatic translations.

3 Methodology

3.1 Research questions

In our analysis we will address several questions related to cohesive devices in English-to-German translations, involving contrastive aspects. These questions are based on the assumptions discussed in relevant works that we described in Section 2 above. We group these questions into three groups: cohesiveness (overall degree of cohesive elements), semantic relations (type of relation used) and variation (variance in data distributions), structuring our analysis (Section 4) according to these.

1. Cohesiveness

    a) How cohesive are the texts in our data?

b) Are there any differences in the degree of cohesion between translated and non-translated texts, and between different translation methods?

2. Semantic relations

   a) Which semantic relations are preferred over others?

   b) Are these preferences language- or production-type-related?

3. Variation

   a) Is there any influence of language variation onto translations resulting in Shining through/Normalisation?

   b) What are the differences between languages, and between translated and non-translated texts in terms of cohesive devices?

3.2 Data

Our corpus data contains both English-German translations texts and non-translated comparable texts in English and German. English originals (EO, source texts) and German originals (GO, comparable texts in the target language) were extracted from CroCo (Hansen-Schirra, Neumann & Steiner 2012). German translations represent multiple translations of EO, and originate from the VARTRA corpus (Lapshinova-Koltunski 2013). They were produced both manually (human translations) and automatically (machine translations). Human translations were produced by both novice and professional translators. Machine-translated texts were produced with different systems: one trained on a small parallel corpus within a restricted domain, and the other one was trained with a huge amount of unknown data[2].

The whole dataset totals 406 texts which cover seven registers: political essays, fictional texts, instruction manuals, popular-scientific articles, letters to shareholders, prepared political speeches, and tourism leaflets. The decision to include this wide range of registers is justified by the need for heterogeneous data for our experiment (as variation is often register-dependent, see Section 2.2 above). However, in this study, we do not take register variation into account. The total number of words comprises ca. 800.000 tokens. We annotate all texts in the corpus with information on word, lemma, part-of-speech, chunk and sentence boundaries with the help of the TreeTagger tools (Schmid 1994).

---

[2] See details on the corpus in Lapshinova-Koltunski (2013).

3.3 Feature extraction

As already mentioned in Section 2.1 above, we concentrate on the analysis of two major categories of cohesive devices: coreference and conjunction. We present these categories in Table 1.

Table 1: Features under analysis

device	type	realisation
coreference	pers.pronoun	he/er, she/sie, they/sie, her/ihr, his/sein, their/ihr, it/es
	dem.pron	this/dies/das, that/jenes, this/diese(r/s), that/jene(r/s), here/hier, there/da, now/jetzt, then/dann, dagegen, damit
	gen.nouns	problem/Problem, situation/Situation, position/Position
conjunction	additive	and/und, for example/zum Beispiel
	adversative	however/allerdings, in contrast/im Gegensatz
	causal	that is why/weshalb, therefore/deswegen
	temporal	then/dann, first/erstens
	modal	interestingly/interessanterweise, of course/natürlich

The first column denotes the category, the second represents their subtypes, and the third illustrates their linguistic realisations (operationalisations) in both English and German. For the extraction of the frequencies of these feature patterns, we use CQP, a corpus query tool (Evert 2005), allowing definition of language patterns in form of regular expressions. These expressions can integrate string, part-of-speech and chunk tags, as well as further constraints, e.g. position in a sentence.

In Table 2, we show examples of the queries for the extraction of personal pronouns (query 1), demonstratives (query 2) and conjunctions (query 3). Queries 1 and 2 contain part-of-speech restrictions only. To further classify them accord-

6 Corpus-based analysis of translation varieties

ing to their functions (modifier vs. head), we use additional queries with such restrictions as (a) position: before a noun phrase ⇒ modifier vs. no noun phrase following ⇒ head (b) lexical restrictions, especially in case of personal pronouns (*he/him* vs. *his*). Query 3 directly includes lexical restrictions – extracted items should be members of the predefined lists, i.e. additive or adversative conjunctions. An example of the lists is given in Table 3.

Table 2: Examples of queries and extracted examples

	QP query	example of extracted pattern
1	[pos="PP.*"]	*sie, ihr, es...*
2	[pos="PD.*"]	*dies/das, jenes, diese(r/s)...*
3	[lemma=RE($additive)]	*darüber hinaus, im Weiteren...*

Table 3: Examples of a lists for conjunctions expressing specific relations

	lexical restrictions
additive	(("(A|a)nd" "also")| ("(A|a)nd" "yet")| ("(F|f)urther")| ("(F|f)urthermore")| ("(M|m)oreover")| ("(I|i)n" "addition")| ("(B|b)esides" "that")| ...)
adversative	(("(A|a)lthough")| ("(H|h)owever")| ("(N|n)evertheless")| ("(D|d)espite" "this")| ("(O|o)n" "the" "other" "hand")| ("(I|i)nstead")| ("(O|o)n" "the" "contrary")| ...)

For the extraction of general nouns, we use queries containing morpho-syntactic restriction such as the one shown in Table 4. We assume that only general nouns within definite noun phrases are cohesive (cf. *this assumption* in example 7 above). Line 1 in Table 4 allows for a definite article. Alternatively, it can be a demonstrative modifier (defined in line 2). The noun itself is defined with lines 3 and 4, where line 3 specifies the part of speech of the searched element, and line 4 redirects the query to the list of predefined lexical items.

Table 4: Example of a query for general nouns

	QP query	explanation
1	[pos="ART"&lemma="d_art"]|	a definite article OR
2	[pos="PDS|PDA.*"]	a demonstrative modifier
3	[pos="NN.*"&	followed by a noun
4	lemma=RE($general)]	whose lemma is a member of predefined list

We illustrate the list of predefined general nouns with an excerpt in Table 5.

Table 5: An excerpt from a query containing a list of general nouns

Part of QP query
[pos="ART"&lemma="account(.*|s)| action(.*|s)| advantag(e|es)| advice| debate(.*|s)| decision(.*|s)| definition(.*|s)| description(.*|s)| discussion(.*|s)| hypothes(i|e)s| idea(.*|s)| issue(.*|s)| matter(.*|s)| message(.*|s)| method(.*|s)| notion(.*|s)| object(.*|s)| observation(.*|s)| opinion(.*|s)| possibilit(y|ies)| problem(.*|s)| scenario(.*|s)|...

With the help of such queries, we collect distributional information on frequencies of cohesive devices per text, and also per subcorpus (e.g. representing a translation variety).

3.4 Methods

For our analysis, a number of visualisation and statistical techniques are applied to investigate the distributional characteristics of subcorpora in terms of occurrences of cohesive devices, described in Section 3.3 above. These descriptive techniques will allow us to observe and explore differences between groups of texts and subcorpora under analysis.

6 Corpus-based analysis of translation varieties

We use both parametric and non-parametric tests. The latter, also called distribution-free tests, do not assume that your data follow a specific distribution. We use box plots, which are non-parametric, to see if there are any differences between the subcorpora under analysis in terms of the overall cohesiveness (Section 4.1). They display variation in samples of a statistical population without making any assumptions about the underlying distributed data (e.g. that it is normally distributed). Box plots are median-oriented graphics used to visualise a summary of the distribution underlying a particular sample. They conveniently depict groups of numerical data through their quartiles (the three points that divide the data set into four equal groups, each group comprising a quarter of the data). Box plots have lines extending vertically from the boxes (*whiskers*), which indicate variability outside the upper and lower quartiles. We use notched box plots to reveal if the differences between variables under analysis are significant. According to Chambers et al. (1983), if two boxes' notches overlap in the box plot, then there is no 'strong evidence' that their medians differ. Alternatively, the difference between the medians could be described as statistically significant at the 0.05 level[3].

Turning to the analysis of concrete features, i.e. semantic relations and those of identity, we use bar plots and line charts for visualisation.

Bar plots present grouped data with rectangular bars to show comparisons among categories. The lengths of the bars is proportional to the values that they represent. One axis of the chart shows the specific categories being compared, and the other axis represents a discrete value. We use bar plots for the visualisation, when not more than two features are involved, e.g. relations of identity vs. logico-semantic ones (Section 4.2), or for the subcategories of the identity relations (Section 4.3.2).

Line plots are used to show frequency of data along a number line. They connect data points of a continuous dependent variable across the levels of an independent variable, illustrating differences across the subcorpora. If the lines are horizontal, there is no difference between the measures compared. Conversely, if there is a slope in the shape of the lines, the subcorpora under analysis show a difference. We use line charts for the analysis of differences based on the distribution of logico-semantic relations, since we have more than two variables at once.

In addition, we apply significance tests to test if the observed differences are significant. For this, we calculate the P-VALUE, which indicates the probability of error or chance in the correlation in our data. The default p-value for the

---

[3] p-value of 0.05, which is commonly used as a bias for significance measure.

difference to be seen as significant is 0.05. So, if the p-value is lower than or equals to 0.05, the probability that the difference between our variables is due to error or chance is lower than or equals to 0.05, so the difference is significant. For the calculation of p-value, we use Pearson's chi-square test and Student's t-test (Baayen 2008) depending on the number of variables in the test set under analysis.

In the following section, we discuss the findings for each of the questions raised at the beginning of Section 3 above.

4 Analyses

4.1 Overall cohesiveness

We measure the overall cohesiveness of the text in our data as the proportion of cohesive tokens (within cohesive features described in 3.3 above) in the total number of tokens per text. Table 6 gives an overview of the minimum, maximum and median values in the four subcorpora under analysis.

Table 6: Overall cohesiveness of EO, GO and translations

	HU	MT	EO	GO
min.	9.78	10.05	9.86	7.95
max.	28.96	27.94	27.57	24.94
median	16.33	15.85	17.44	17.42

As seen from the table, the English and German originals seem to be similar (if the median values are taken into account) in terms of the overall cohesiveness. This contradicts the findings by (Kunz et al. 2017: 22), who observe more cohesive devices in the German texts than in the English ones in their data. On the one hand, the discrepancy in the results can be explained by the definition of the features under analysis. While we use automatically induced cohesive devices, Kunz et al. (*forthcoming*) operate with manually annotated data. On the other hand, we believe that the cohesiveness values can strongly depend on the texts in a dataset, i.e. cross-lingual cohesiveness in Kunz et al. (*forthcoming*) varies depending on the text registers involved: it is higher for English, if fictional texts and those published on corporate websites are considered. The influence of text variability is also reflected in the minimum and maximum values in the subcorpora, see Table 6, with German originals revealing the lowest ones. The highest maximum value and the lowest minimum value are observed in both translation varieties. However, they also demonstrate a lower proportion of cohesive items in terms of the median value, which means that in general, we observe a reduction of cohesiveness in translation, with machine translation showing the lowest values. This contradicts the phenomenon of explicitation – tendency to spell things out rather than leave them implicit. Assuming that cohesive devices help to explicate coherence relations in a text, we would expect translated texts to be more cohesive than non-translated ones. However, we believe that in this case, we would not need to pay attention to all devices taken together, but to distributions of individual phenomena, e.g. conjunctions expressing logico-semantic relations, or proportion of head vs. modifier functions of pronouns. Moreover, a direct comparison of concrete source texts vs. target texts is also required.

Overall, the median values in Table 6 suggest that the difference between the four subcorpora in our data is not big. We test its significance producing boxplots illustrated in Figure 1. As explained in Section 3.4 above, if two boxes' notches do not overlap, we can observe a significant difference between their medians.

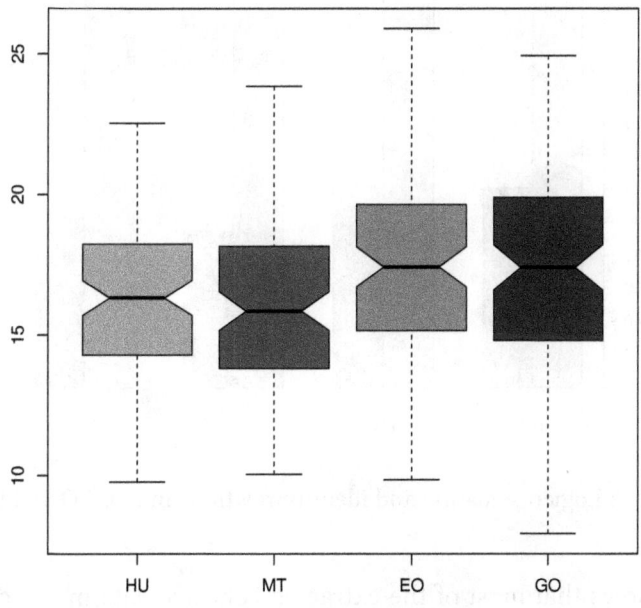

Figure 1: Overall cohesiveness of EO, GO and translations

Analysing notches for the four subcorpora in our data, we see that there is no significant difference between EO and GO, as well as between HT and MT in terms of cohesiveness. Translations (especially machine ones) do differ from non-translated texts, which conforms to the insights from other studies on translationese.

4.2 Semantic relations

In this section, we analyse the distribution of cohesive relations in our data. We start by looking at the distributions for the two main categories: devices signaling identity and devices signaling all types of logico-semantic relations taken together, see Figure 2.

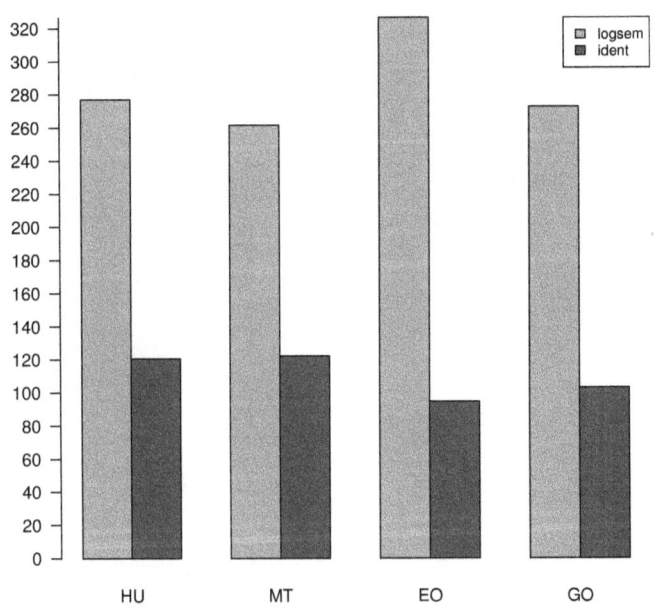

Figure 2: Logico-semantic and identity relations in EO, GO and translations

Figure 2 shows that most of the extracted cohesive data in our corpus is represented by items expressing logico-semantic relations. English texts are characterised by the highest number of logico-semantic devices and the lowest number of linguistic means expressing identity. This contradicts again the results by (Kunz et al. 2017: 25). This discrepancy can be explained by the difference in the definition of conjunctive devices. Ours also include subjuncts which were excluded from the analysis described by (Kunz et al. 2017).

Both translation varieties tend to be similar to German texts. Significance analysis with Pearson's Chi-squared test confirms this observation. The only significant differences (p < 0.05) are observed for the pairs EO vs. HT (p=0.01) and EO vs. MT (p=0.004).

In terms of specific logico-semantic relations, we observe a preference for additive and causal relations in English texts, and for additive and temporal relations for all texts in German (including translations and originals). In this way, our results show that preferences for semantic relations observed in our data are rather language-specific, as translated texts show similarities to comparable non-translated originals in German.

4.3 Variation

In the following, we concentrate on linguistic means expressing cohesion, and their variation across subcorpora under analysis.

4.3.1 Logico-semantic relations

We calculate type-token-ratio (TTR) for cohesive expressions of logico-semantic relations (note that we understand a single occurrence of a conjunctive phrase as a token in this case), see Table 7.

Table 7: Cohesive types expressing logico-semantic relations

	types	tokens	TTR
HU	340	29669	1.15
MT	266	27411	0.97
EO	180	36904	0.49
GO	592	32709	1.81

Although English texts demonstrate the highest number of cohesive items expressing logico-semantic relations, they do not contain many types of conjunctive words. This coincides with general observations on English and German vocabulary, as well as our previous findings (Kunz & Lapshinova-Koltunski 2014), where we also show that the TTR in the German originals exceeds that of the English ones, thus finding a higher degree of variation in the German data. Not surprisingly, both translation varieties reveal a lower degree of variation with a lower TTR. Significance analysis with the help of Student's t-Test shows that the difference between the four subcorpora in terms of TTR is not significant.

Table 8: Ranking of frequent cohesive conjunctions

HT		MT		GO		EO	
7601	und	7939	und	7601	und	12031	as
1225	um	1100	oder	1317	auch	898	because
1162	als	1097	um	1120	als	575	since
995	oder	1004	als	942	oder	459	although
844	wie	879	wie	849	wie	237	but

If we take a look at the five most frequent types (see Table 8), we can see that one main cause for the variance between English and German texts is the high number of occurrences of *as* in EO[4]. Interestingly, the German lists of conjunctions demonstrate discrepancy between non-translated and translated German (*um* in translations, and *auch* in the original German texts). The top three conjunctions in English also explain the preferences for causal relations that we observed in Section 4.2 above.

We must admit that application of fully automatic procedures to extract the data leaves us at the mercy of the tool and the tag set. The TreeTagger does not distinguish between prepositions and subordinating conjunctions which might seriously distort the results concerning conjunction. However, we have to accept these results provided the fact that extractions from all subcorpora under analysis were performed automatically.

4.3.2 Identity via coreference

For identity relations via pronouns, we compare the distributions of their grammatical functions (as a modifier or a head) in all subcorpora under analysis. Figure 3 illustrates functional preferences for coreference with demonstrative pronouns in English, German, and both translation varieties[5].

German texts show the lowest number of modifiers out of all analysed subcorpora, whereas both translation varieties demonstrate a declining number of

---

[4] Please note that our list can also contain cases of non-cohesive *as*, since all features are extracted with automatic procedures.

[5] The numbers are given in % normalised per total number of tokens.

6 *Corpus-based analysis of translation varieties*

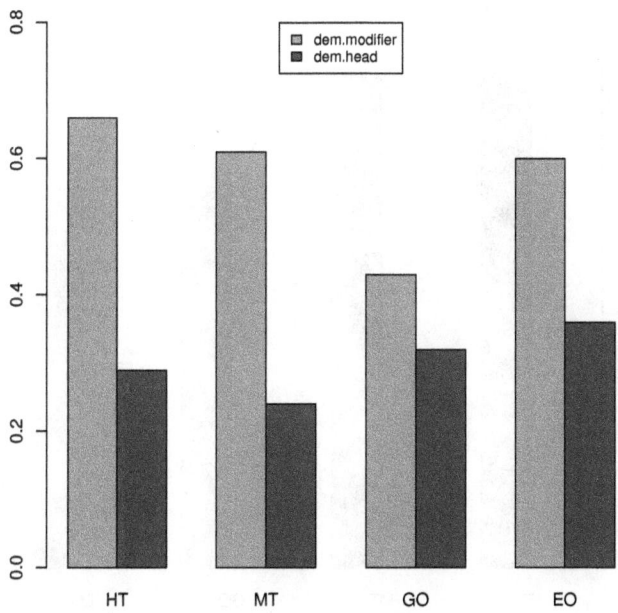

Figure 3: Functional preferences of demonstrative reference

heads[6]. At the same time, we find the highest number of modifiers in translations (with human translation on the top). We assume that this tendency in translation follows from the process of explicitation (see Section 4.1): modifiers that precede a noun or a noun phrase are more explicit means for expressing identity relations than demonstrative pronouns as heads, compare (8) and (9).

(8) *Etwas gerät in Bewegung, und <u>diese</u> Bewegung hält an.* ("Something gets set in motion and this motion continues").

(9) *Etwas gerät in Bewegung, und <u>diese</u> hält an.* ("Something gets set in motion and this continues").

At the same time, it is surprising that translations in our data also demonstrate the highest number of personal heads, as seen in Figure 4.

Analysing variation in the subcorpora with Pearson's Chi-squared test, we find a significant difference between all subcorpora in terms of both personal and

---

[6] Note that we did not take into account pronominal adverbs, e.g. *darüber*, which also function as heads, as well as definite articles functioning as modifiers.

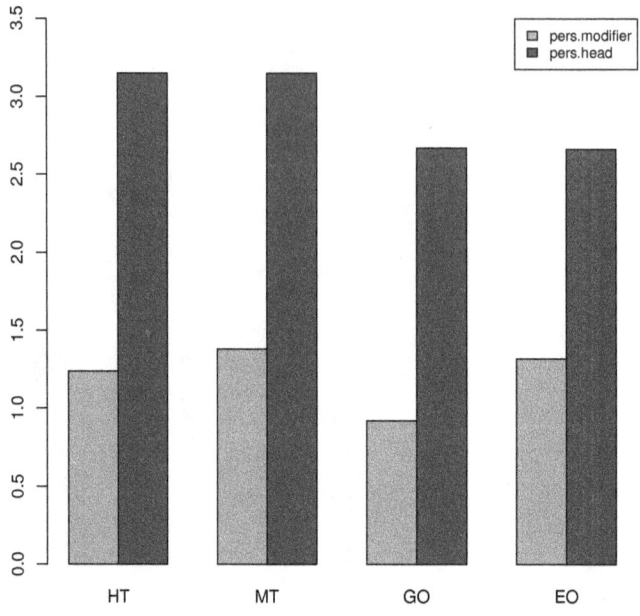

Figure 4: Functional preferences of personal reference

demonstrative reference. The only exception is the distribution of demonstrative modifiers and heads in both translation varieties: human and machine translation apparently do not differ significantly.

In the last step, we compare the type-token-ratio of general nouns. The values for both translation types turn out to be higher than for non-translated subcorpora.

Table 9: General nouns expressing identity relations

	types	tokens	TTR
HT	65	280	23.21
MT	55	191	28.80
GO	99	601	16.47
EO	122	575	21.22

This is surprising, as translations are supposed to have lower TTR than originals (as stated by Hansen-Schirra, Neumann & Steiner 2012). Apart from that, general nouns belong to the most frequent words of the vocabulary. Thus, their higher number in translations might be an indicator of simplification (tendency to simplify the language used in translation).

In Table 10, we present the most frequent general nouns occurring in our data. It is interesting to see that translations share the most frequent general nouns with both source texts (marked with light blue) and comparable texts in the target language (marked with dark blue). We also observe some cases that are common in both English and German texts (marked with light green), as well as words shared by translations only (marked with dark green).

Table 10: Most frequent general nouns

HT	MT	GO	EO
Ziel	Ziel	Frage	system
Weise	Bereich	Ziel	area
Bereich	Problem	Entwicklung	information
Grund	System	Möglichkeit	case
Problem	Ergebnis	Weg	result
System	Frage	Fall	message
Veränderung	Weise	Geschichte	story
Weg	Schritt	Bereich	problem
Ding	Bericht	Prozess	thing
Frage	Punkt	Art	point

Interestingly, human translations share the same number of frequent general nouns with both English and German, whereas machine translations contain more nouns occurring in the English source texts. This is interpreted as a sign of stronger shining through in MT. The word *Weise* shared by both translation varieties is semantically related to *Art* (*Weise* and *Art* are synonyms), one of the most frequent general nouns in German originals texts.

5 Conclusion and discussion

In this paper, we have analysed cohesive properties of multilingual texts that contain both translated and non-translated texts using descriptive techniques. The results show that these properties vary depending on the languages and text production types involved. Languages, even such closely related ones as English and German, have different preferences in the usage of cohesive devices. The observed variation in translations is also influenced by the method involved. Both human and machine translations have constellations of cohesive devices different from those of their underlying originals, and from comparable non-translated texts in the target language. Comparing texts in two translation varieties with original texts in the source or the target language, we found that differences between the two translation varieties are smaller than between translated and original texts. This is not surprising, as parallel data used in the MT development contains human translations. This intensifies levelling out or convergence. We observed this tendency for various features, e.g. for the overall cohesiveness of texts, logico-semantic relations and partly for the relations of identity.

Translations seem to demonstrate explicitation as well, for instance in terms of grammatical functions of cohesive reference via demonstrative pronouns. At the same time, we could not find this for all cohesive devices under analysis taken together. Here, we observed signs of normalisation instead. We could also detect shining through effects, i.e. in terms of general nouns, especially in machine translation.

Overall, our results partly coincide with the observation in our previous analyses: for instance, in our study on shallow features (Lapshinova-Koltunski 2015b), in the one on register-based features (Lapshinova-Koltunski 2017) or the study in which we used discourse-related feature set (Lapshinova-Koltunski 2015a) but applied automatic classification techniques.

At the same time, we realise that there are some limitations of our approach, especially in terms of features under analysis. The frequencies of the cohesive devices were obtained in a completely automatic annotation and query approach. Therefore, on the basis of our findings, we cannot conclude that the processes observed are specific for English and German in general. However, this approach is sufficient for the analysis of differences between the subcorpora at hand, since the features were automatically extracted from all of them.

In the future, it would be interesting to see if the differences between translated and original texts affect perception of the quality of the text as received by humans, for which experiments involving human judgements are required. Moreover, we would like to apply the knowledge on the discrepancies in cohesive devices between human and machine translations, as well as between English and German texts to machine translation, including both MT development and MT evaluation.

Acknowledgments

This paper is based on corpus resources built up in the framework of the VARTRA project[7] which was funded through *Anschubfinanzierung* of Saarland University. We thank our anonymous reviewers for their constructive comments. We also gratefully acknowledge the help of editors in preparing the final version of this article. All remaining errors and misconceptions are our own.

References

Baayen, R. Harald. 2008. *Analyzing linguistic data. A practical introduction to statistics using R*. Cambridge: Cambridge University Press.

Baker, Mona. 1993. Corpus linguistics and translation studies: Implications and applications. In Mona Baker, Gill Francis & Elena Tognini-Bonelli (eds.), *Text and Technology: In honour of John Sinclair*, 233–250. Amsterdam: Benjamins.

Baker, Mona. 1995. Corpora in translation studies: An overview and some suggestions for future research. *Target* 7(2). 223–243.

Becher, Viktor. 2011. *Explicitation and implicitation in translation. A corpus-based study of English-German and German-English translations of business texts*. Universität Hamburg PhD thesis.

Bisiada, Mario. 2014. Lösen Sie Schachtelsätze möglichst auf: The impact of editorial guidelines on sentence splitting in German business article translations. *Applied Linguistics* 3.

Blum-Kulka, Shoshana. 1986. Shifts of cohesion and coherence in translation. In Juliane House & Shoshana Blum-Kulka (eds.), *Interlingual and intercultural communication*, 17–35. Tübingen: Gunter Narr.

Bührig, Kristin & Juliane House. 2004. Connectivity in translation: Transitions from orality to literacy. In J. House & J. Rehbein (eds.), *Multilingual communication*, 87–114. Amsterdam: Benjamins.

Chambers, John M., William S. Cleveland, Beat Kleiner & Paul A. Tukey. 1983. *Graphical methods for data analysis* (The Wadsworth Statistics/Probability Series). Boston: Duxbury Press.

Doherty, Monica. 2004. Strategy of incremental parsimony. *SPRIKreports* (25).

Evert, Stefan. 2005. *The CQP query language tutorial*. CWB version 2.2.b90. IMS Stuttgart.

---

[7] http://fedora.clarin-d.uni-saarland.de/vartra/

Fabricius-Hansen, Cathrine. 1999. Information packaging and translation: Aspects of translational sentence splitting (German–English/Norwegian). *Studia Grammatica* 47. 175–214.

Gellerstam, Martin. 1986. Translationese in Swedish novels translated from English. In L. Wollin & H. Lindquist (eds.), *Translation studies in Scandinavia*, 88–95. Lund: CWK Gleerup.

Guillou, Liane. 2012. Improving pronoun translation for statistical machine translation. In *EACL 2012, 13th Conference of the European Chapter of the Association for Computational Linguistics, Avignon, France, April 23-27, 2012*, 1–10.

Guillou, Liane. 2013. Analysing lexical consistency in translation. In *Proceedings of the Workshop on Discourse in Machine Translation*, 10–18. Sofia, Bulgaria: Association for Computational Linguistics. http://www.aclweb.org/anthology/W13-3302.

Halliday, Michael A. K. & Ruqaiya Hasan. 1976. *Cohesion in English*. London: Longman Publishing.

Halliday, Michael A. K. & Christian Matthiessen. 2004. *Introduction to functional grammar*. 3rd edition. London: Arnold.

Halliday, Michael A. K. & Christian Matthiessen. 2013. *Halliday's introduction to functional grammar*. London: Routledge.

Hansen-Schirra, Silvia, Stella Neumann & Erich Steiner. 2012. *Cross-linguistic corpora for the study of translations. Insights from the language pair English-German*. Berlin, New York: de Gruyter.

Hardmeier, Christian. 2012. Discourse in statistical machine translation. A survey and a case study. *Discours* 11. Caen.

Hardmeier, Christian. 2014. *Discourse in statistical machine translation*. Uppsala: Acta Universitatis Upsaliensis PhD thesis.

Kunz, Kerstin & Ekaterina Lapshinova-Koltunski. 2014. Cohesive conjunctions in English and German: Systemic contrasts and textual differences. In Vandelanotte Lieven, Kristin Davidse, Caroline Gentens & Ditte Kimps (eds.), *Recent advances in corpus linguistics: Developing and exploiting corpora*, vol. 78 (Language and Computers - Studies in Practical Linguistics), 229–262. Amsterdam/New York: Rodopi.

Kunz, Kerstin & Ekaterina Lapshinova-Koltunski. 2015. Cross-linguistic analysis of discourse variation across registers. *Nordic Journal of English Studies* 14(1). K. Ajmer & H. Hassegard (eds.). 258–288.

Kunz, Kerstin, Stefania Degaetano-Ortlieb, Ekaterina Lapshinova-Koltunski, Katrin Menzel & Erich Steiner. 2017. GECCo – an empirically-based comparison of English-German cohesion. In G. De Sutter, I. Delaere & M.-A. Lefer (eds.),

New ways of analysing translational behaviour in corpus-based translation studies. TILSM series. Berlin: Mouton de Gruyter.

Lapshinova-Koltunski, Ekaterina. 2013. VARTRA: A comparable corpus for analysis of translation variation. In *Proceedings of the 6th Workshop on Building and Using Comparable Corpora*, 77–86. Sofia, Bulgaria: Association for Computational Linguistics. http://www.aclweb.org/anthology/W13-2510.

Lapshinova-Koltunski, Ekaterina. 2015a. Exploration of inter- and intralingual variation of discourse phenomen. In *Proceedings of EMNLP 2015 Workshop on Discourse in Machine Translation*. Lisbon.

Lapshinova-Koltunski, Ekaterina. 2015b. Variation in translation: Evidence from corpora. In Claudio Fantinuoli & Federico Zanettin (eds.), *New directions in corpus-based translation studies* (Translation and Multilingual Natural Language Processing), 93–113. Berlin: Language Science Press.

Lapshinova-Koltunski, Ekaterina. 2017. Exploratory analysis of dimensions influencing variation in translation: The case of text register and translation method. In G. De Sutter, I. Delaere & M.-A. Lefer (eds.), *New Ways of Analysing Translational Behaviour in Corpus-Based Translation Studies*. TILSM series. Berlin: Mouton de Gruyter.

Lapshinova-Koltunski, Ekaterina & Kerstin Kunz. 2014. Conjunctions across languages, registers and modes: Semi-automatic extraction and annotation. In A. Diaz Negrillo & J. Daz-Pérez Francesco (eds.), *Specialisation and variation in language corpora* (Linguistic Insights 179), 77–104. Frankfurt: Peter Lang.

Laviosa-Braithwaite, Sara. 2002. *Corpus-based translation studies, theory, findings, application*. Amsterdam: Rodopi.

Li, Junyi Jessy, Marine Carpuat & Ani Nenkova. 2014a. Assessing the discourse factors that influence the quality of machine translation. In *Proceedings of the 52nd Annual Meeting of the Association for Computational Linguistics (Volume 2: Short Papers)*, 283–288. Baltimore, Maryland: Association for Computational Linguistics. http://www.aclweb.org/anthology/P14-2047.

Li, Junyi Jessy, Marine Carpuat & Ani Nenkova. 2014b. Cross-lingual discourse relation analysis: A corpus study and a semi-supervised classification system. In *Proceedings of COLING 2014, the 25th International Conference on Computational Linguistics: Technical Papers*, 577–587. Dublin, Ireland.

Mascarell, Laura, Mark Fishel, Natalia Korchagina & Martin Volk. 2014. Enforcing consistent translation of German compound coreferences. In *Proceedings of KONVENS 2014*. s.n. DOI:http://dx.doi.org/10.5167/uzh-98540

Meyer, Thomas, Najeh Hajlaoui & Andrei Popescu-Belis. 2015. Disambiguating discourse connectives for statistical machine translation. *Audio, Speech, and Language Processing, IEEE/ACM Transactions* 23(7). 1184–1197.

Meyer, Thomas & Bonnie Webber. 2013. Implicitation of discourse connectives in (machine) translation. In *Proceedings of the Workshop on Discourse in Machine Translation*, 19–26. Sofia, Bulgaria: Association for Computational Linguistics. http://www.aclweb.org/anthology/W13-3303.

Schmid, Helmut. 1994. Probabilistic part-of-speech tagging using decision trees. In *International conference on new methods in language processing*, 44–49. Manchester, UK.

Taboada, Maite & María de los Ángeles Gómez-González. 2012. Discourse markers and coherence relations: Comparison across markers, languages and modalities. *Linguistics and the Human Sciences* 6(1–3). 17–41.

Teich, Elke. 2003. *Cross-linguistic variation in system and text. A methodology for the investigation of translations and comparable texts.* Berlin: Mouton de Gruyter.

Vinay, Jean P. & Jean Darbelnet. 1958. *Stylistique comparée du français et de l'anglais. Méthode de traduction.* Paris: Didier.

Webber, Bonnie, Andrei Popescu-Belis, Katja Markert & Jörg Tiedemann (eds.). 2013. *Proceedings of the Workshop on Discourse in Machine Translation.* Sofia, Bulgaria: Association for Computational Linguistics. http://www.aclweb.org/anthology/W13-33.

Zinsmeister, Heike, Stefanie Dipper & Melanie Seiss. 2012. Abstract pronominal anaphors and label nouns in German and English: Selected case studies and quantitative investigations. *Translation: Computation, Corpora, Cognition* 2(1). http://www.t-c3.org/index.php/t-c3/article/view/16.

Chapter 7

Examining lexical coherence in a multilingual setting

Karin Sim Smith
The University of Sheffield

Lucia Specia
The University of Sheffield

> This paper presents a preliminary study of lexical coherence and cohesion in the context of multiple languages. We explore two entity-based frameworks in a multilingual setting in an attempt to understand how lexical coherence is realised across different languages. These frameworks (an entity-grid model and an entity graph metric) have previously been used for assessing coherence in a monolingual setting. We apply them to a multilingual setting for the first time, assessing whether entity based coherence frameworks could help ensure lexical coherence in a Machine Translation context.

1 Introduction

We present an exploratory study which represents our early research on how lexical coherence is realised in a multilingual context, with a view to identifying patterns that could be later used to improve overall translation quality in Machine Translation (MT) models.

Ideally a coherent source document when translated properly should result in a coherent target document. Coherence does vary in how it is achieved in different languages. Moreover, unlike a human translator, who translates the document as a whole, in context, ensuring that the translated document is as coherent as the source document, most MT systems, and particularly Statistical

Karin Sim Smith & Lucia Specia. 2017. Examining lexical coherence in a multilingual setting. In Katrin Menzel, Ekaterina Lapshinova-Koltunski & Kerstin Kunz (eds.), *New perspectives on cohesion and coherence*, 119–137. Berlin: Language Science Press. DOI:10.5281/zenodo.814470

Machine Translation (SMT) systems, translate each sentence in isolation, and have no notion of discourse principles such as coherence and cohesion.

While some research has indicated that MT frameworks are good at lexical cohesion (Carpuat & Simard 2012), in that they are consistent, others have reported different results (Wong & Kit 2012), since MT systems can persist using with a particular translation which is incorrect. We believe that investigating entity-based frameworks in a multilingual setting may shed some light on the issue. In particular, we also hope to ascertain whether they help in the disambiguation of lexical entities, where in an MT setting the translation of a particular source word, e.g. 'bank' in English, could be translated as either 'la rive' or 'la banque' in French, depending on the context. Currently most SMT systems determine which word to use purely based on the probabilities established at training time (i.e. how frequently 'bank' equated to 'la rive' and how frequently it equated to 'la banque'). While, this should be determined by context, the problem is that most systems translate one sentence at a time, disregarding the wider context.

Greater insight into how multilingual lexical coherence is achieved could lead to improvements in current translation approaches. This improvement could take the form of features based on the entity transitions, guiding the lexical choice. Alternatively, we could use coherence models to select the option which leads to a higher translation score when reranking results from a decoder.

In the following (Section 2) we describe entity based coherence. We briefly explain the grid model (Section 3) and the graph one (Section 4). Then we detail our experimental settings (Section 5) for the two main parts of this research. Firstly (Section 6), we constructed a multilingual comparative entity-based GRID for a corpus comprising various documents covering three different languages. We examine whether similar patterns of entity transitions are exhibited, or whether they varied markedly across languages. Secondly (Section 7), we applied an entity **graph** in a multilingual context, using the same corpus. We assess whether this different perspective offers more insight into crosslingual coherence patterns. Our conclusions are set out in Section 8. Our goals are to understand differences in lexical coherence across languages so that in the future we can establish whether this can be used as a means of ensuring that the appropriate level of lexical coherence is transferred from source to machine translated documents.

2 Entity-based coherence

There has been recent work in the area of lexical cohesion in MT (Xiong et al. 2013a,b; Tiedemann 2010; Hardmeier 2012; Carpuat & Simard 2012; Wong & Kit

2012), as a sub category of coherence, looking at the linguistic elements which hold a text together. However, there seems to be little work in the wider area of coherence as a whole. Coherence is indeed a more complex discourse element to define in the first place. While it does include cohesion, it is wider in terms of also describing how a text becomes semantically meaningful overall, and how easy it is for the reader to follow.

Xiong et al. (2013b) focus on ensuring lexical cohesion by reinforcing the choice of lexical items during decoding. They subsequently compute lexical chains in the source text (Xiong et al. 2013a), project these onto the target text, and integrate these into the decoding process with different strategies. This is to try and ensure that the lexical cohesion, as represented through the choice of lexical items, is transferred from the source to target text. Tiedemann (2010) attempts to improve lexical consistency and to adapt statistical models to be more linguistically sensitive, integrating contextual dependencies by means of a dynamic cache model. Hardmeier (2012) suggests there is not much to be gained by just enforcing consistent vocabulary choice in SMT, since the vocabulary is already fairly consistent. While there is indeed a case for arguing that MT systems can be more consistent than human translators for using a set terminology (Carpuat & Simard 2012), that would only be valid for a very narrow field, perhaps a highly technical domain, and an SMT system trained on exact data. Wong & Kit (2012) study lexical cohesion as a means of evaluating the quality of MT output at document level, but in their case the focus is on it as an evaluation metric. Their research supports the intuition we found, i.e. that human translators intuitively ensure cohesion, which in MT output often is represented as direct translations of source text items that may be inappropriate in the target context. They conclude that MT needs to learn to use lexical cohesion devices appropriately.

Lexical cohesion is only one aspect of coherence, however much of the work on computationally determining how lexical cohesion is indicative of coherence refers to 'coherence', therefore we retain the term 'coherence' here, as we are looking at how lexical cohesion contributes to coherence as a whole. In particular, the focus, or the 'attentional state' (Grosz & Sidner 1986) in a discourse is one major aspect of coherence. Entity-based coherence aims to measure the attentional state, formalised via Centering Theory (Grosz, Weinstein & Joshi 1995) (more below).

The entity-based approach was first proposed by Barzilay & Lapata (2005) with the aim of measuring local coherence in a monolingual setting, focusing on applications where multiple alternatives of a system output are available, such as the ranking of alternative automatic text summaries by their coherence degree.

As detailed by Barzilay & Lapata (2008), the entity-based approach derives from the theory that entities in a coherent text are distributed in a certain manner, as identified in various discourse theories, in particular in Centering Theory (Grosz, Weinstein & Joshi 1995). This theory holds that coherent texts are characterised by salient entities in strong grammatical roles, such as subject or object. The focus of their work (Barzilay & Lapata 2008) was in using this knowledge, via patterns in terms of prominent syntactic constructions, to distinguish coherent from non-coherent texts. In our research the focus is on differences in the general patterns, particularly across languages. As long as a syntactic parser is available, this approach is fully automatic and avoids human annotation effort. We see it as a means of extracting additional linguistic information for use in rich features to guide lexical selection in MT, as well as potentially in the problem of MT evaluation.

Previous computational models for assessing coherence have been deployed in a monolingual setting (Lapata 2005; Barzilay & Lapata 2008; Elsner, Austerweil & Charniak 2007; Elsner & Charniak 2011; Burstein, Tetreault & Andreyev 2010; Guinaudeau & Strube 2013). We report on our findings for applying the entity grid (Section 6) and entity graph (Section 7) to a multilingual setting, using data and settings as described in Section 5.

Our initial experiments will take all nouns in the document as discourse entities, as recommended by Elsner & Charniak (2011), and investigate how they are realised crosslingually. The distribution of entities over sentences may vary from language to language (more on this below). The challenge from an MT point of view would be to ensure that an entity chain is carried over to from source to target text, despite differences in syntax and sentence structure, and taking account of linguistic variations.

3 Entity grid

Entity distribution patterns vary according to text domain, style and genre, which are all valuable characteristics to capture, and attempt to transfer from source to target text languages where appropriate. They are constructed by identifying the discourse entities in the documents under consideration and representing them in 2D grids whereby each column corresponds to the entity, i.e. noun, being tracked, and each row represents a particular sentence in the document in order. An example can be seen in Table 1, where the lines represent consecutive sentences, and the columns ('e1', etc.) represent different entities. In this example, 'e7' represents 'Kosovo', which was repeated in sentences 's2', 's3' and 's4', in the roles of *subject* (S), *other* (X), and *subject* (S), respectively.

7 Examining lexical coherence in a multilingual setting

Table 1: Example of entity grid

	e1	e2	e3	e4	e5	e6	e7
s1	-	-	-	-	-	-	-
s2	-	-	-	-	-	-	S
s3	-	-	-	-	-	-	X
s4	-	-	O	-	-	-	S
s5	S	-	-	-	-	-	-
s6	-	-	-	X	-	-	-

Once all occurrences of nouns and the syntactic roles they represent in each sentence (Subject (S), Object (O), or other (X)) are extracted, an ENTITY TRANSITION is defined as a consecutive occurrence of an entity, with given syntactic roles. These are computed by examining the grid vertically for each entity. For example, an 'SS', a 'Subject-to-Subject' transition, indicates that an entity occurs in a subject position in two consecutive sentences. An 'SO', on the other hand, indicates that while the entity was in a subject role in one sentence, it became the object in the subsequent sentence. Probabilities for these transitions can be easily derived by calculating the frequency of a particular transition divided by the total number of transitions which occur in that document.

4 Entity graph

Guinaudeau & Strube (2013) projected the entity grid into a graph format, using a bipartite graph which they claim had the advantage both of avoiding the data sparsity issues encountered by Barzilay & Lapata (2008) and of achieving equal performance on measuring overall document coherence without the need for training. They use it to capture the same entity transition information as the entity grid experiment, although they only track the occurrence of entities, avoiding the nulls or absences of the other (tracked as '-' in the entity grid framework). Additionally, the graph representation can track cross-sentential references, instead of only those in adjacent sentences (Guinaudeau & Strube 2013).

The graph tracks the presence of all entities, taking all nouns in the document as discourse entities, as recommended by Elsner & Charniak (2011), and connections to the sentences they occur in. The general form of the coherence score assigned to a document in this approach is shown in Equation 7.1. This is a centrality measure based on the average outdegree across the N sentences represented in the document graph. The outdegree of a sentence s_i, denoted $o(s_i)$, is the total weight leaving that sentence, a notion of how connected (or how central) it is. This weight is the sum of the contributions of all edges connecting s_i to any $s_j \in D$.

$$s(D) = \frac{1}{N} \sum_{i=1}^{N} o(s_i) \qquad (7.1)$$

$$= \frac{1}{N} \sum_{i=1}^{N} \sum_{j=i+1}^{N} W_{i,j}$$

The coherence of a text in this model is measured by calculating the average outdegree of a projection, so by summing the shared edges (i.e. of entities leaving a sentence) between two sentences.

They define three types of graph projections: *binary*, *weighted* and *syntactic*. Binary projections simply record whether two sentences have any entities in common. Weighted projections take the number of shared entities into account, rating the projections higher for more shared entities. A syntactic projection includes syntax information, where syntactic information is used to weight the importance of the link by calculating an entity in role of subject (S) as a 3, an entity in role of object (O) as a 2, and other (X) as a 1. These are projected between any two sentences in the text, as sets of shared entities.

We projected the entity relationships onto a graph-based representation, as per Guinaudeau & Strube (2013), experimenting in various settings. Our objective was to assess whether the graph gives us a better appreciation of differences in entity-based coherence across languages. This representation can encode more information than the entity-grid as it spans connections not just between adjacent sentences, but among all sentences in the document.

5 Experimental settings

For our multilingual experiments, the entity grid approach was applied to parallel texts from the WMT corpus,[1] with three languages: English, French, and German. In particular, we used the test data, comprising news excerpts extracted over various years. The direction of translation varies for different documents, as discussed in Section 6. For comparison, we also take the French and English documents from the **LIG** corpus (Potet et al. 2012) of French into English translations. These form a concatenated group of 361 documents, which are news

---

[1] http://www.statmt.org/wmt10/

excerpts drawn from various WMT years. In all these corpora, translations are provided by human, professional translators.

French to English is generally regarded as a well performing language pair in MT, whereas German to English is more error-prone due to compounding, word order and morphological variations in German. Of particular interest here are the compound words prevalent in German, and how these affect the entity grid. To establish general tendencies, entity grids were compiled for three different sources:

- The **newstest2008** datasets in each language comprising 90 parallel documents.
- The **LIG** corpus in French and English comprising 361 parallel documents.

In our experiments we used version 3.3.0 of the Stanford Parser[2] to identify the noun phrases in each language. We set the salience at 2, i.e. recording only entities which occurred more than twice, and derived models with transitions of length 3 (i.e. over 3 adjacent sentences). We computed the mean of the transition probabilities, i.e. the probability of a particular transition occurring, over all the documents.

While previous work for English, a language with a relatively fixed word order, has found factors such as the grammatical roles associated with the entities affect local coherence, this varies across languages (Cheung & Penn 2010). Cheung & Penn (2010) further suggest that topological fields (identifying clausal structure in terms of the positions of different constituents) are an alternative to grammatical roles in local coherence modelling, for languages such as German, and show that they are superior to grammatical roles in an ordering experiment.

For this set of experiments we therefore apply a slightly simplified version of the grid, recording the presence or absence of particular (salient) entities over a sequence of sentences. In addition to being the first cross-lingual study of the grid approach, this experiment also aims at examining the robustness of this approach without a syntactic parser. While the grammatical function may have been useful as an indicator in the aforementioned work, this does not necessarily hold in a multilingual context. Simply tracking the existence or absence of entities allows for direct comparison across languages. Indeed, as Filippova & Strube (2007) reported when applying the entity grid approach to group related entities and incorporate semantic relatedness, "syntactic information turned out to have a negative impact on the results". While Barzilay & Lapata (2008) argued that "the proposed representation reveals entity transition patterns characteristic of coherent texts", we would also suggest that these patterns potentially vary

---

[2] http://nlp.stanford.edu/software/corenlp.shtml

from language to language to some extent, while retaining an overall degree of coherence.

6 Multilingual grids

6.1 In-depth analysis

In order to illustrate the differences between the distributions of entity transitions over the different languages, we computed Jensen-Shannon divergence scores for French and English, and then German and English, both displayed in Figure 1.

Paying attention to the scale, it is clear that the German and English divergence is greater overall than the divergence for French and English. For example the entity transitions which showed the highest variation were $XX-$, which was 0.045 for the difference between French and English over 0.1 for German and English, also transition XXX where the difference over the same was 0.02 and 0.08. This indicates that for the German-English pair it was less likely that the same entity showed up in 3 consecutive sentences than for the French-English pair.

Table 2: Multilingual entity transitions (mean of 90 documents)

Transition	German	French	English
'XXX'	0.001445	0.002382	0.000441
'X-X'	0.006240	0.006917	0.003184
'XX-'	0.005905	0.008853	0.003130
'-XX'	0.004142	0.006155	0.001672

While German is more nominal in structure, and one might expect higher entity transition probabilities in general, these are often compound nouns, which are then counted separately in our setup. This variance merits more investigation to gain a fuller picture of the reasons behind it.

There is a clear pattern across the entity transitions over the three languages studied. In this instance we are comparing the same texts, on a document by document basis, so the same genre and style, yet there is a consistent difference in the probabilities. This would appear to indicate, amongst other things, that the manner in which lexical coherence is achieved varies from language to language.

7 Examining lexical coherence in a multilingual setting

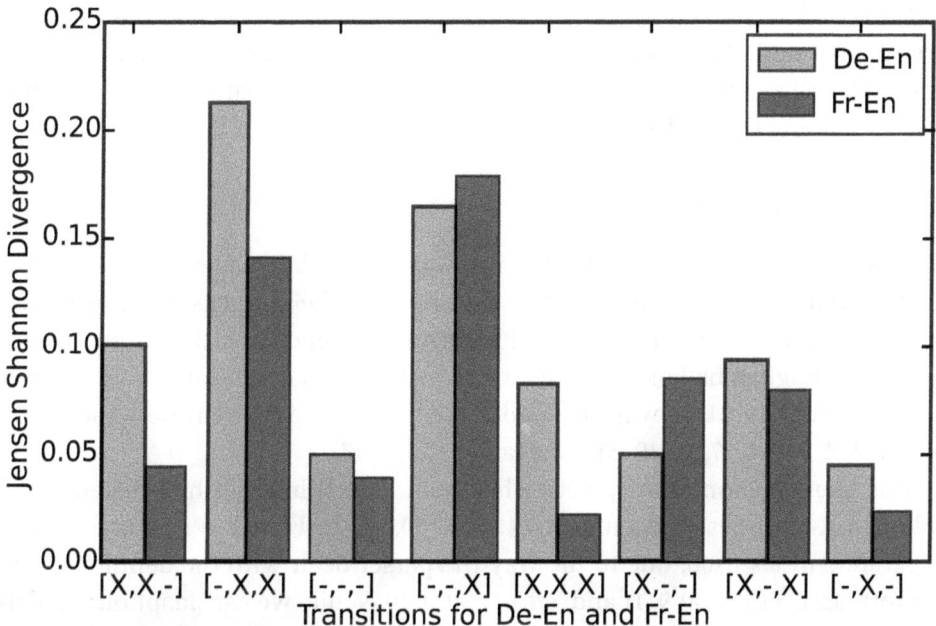

Figure 1: Jensen-Shannon divergence over distribution of entity transitions (length 3) for German-English and French-English (WMT newstest2008)

While this is just a preliminary study with a small dataset, this is supported by other research findings (Lapshinova-Koltunski 2015b).

On closer analysis, it would appear that there are various issues at play. Firstly, there is the matter of sentence boundaries, which affects the transition probabilities. Across many of the documents in the **newstest2008**, the French version had fewer sentences within segments than the corresponding segments in German or English. This potentially increases the number of transitions from sentence to sentence. French also exhibited on average fewer entities per document. So the transitions are more concentrated. Both of these factors potentially account for some of the higher levels of entity transitions in French over English and German in the WMT **newstest2008** documents.

The tendency in the WMT **newstest2008** documents was for English and German to have more, shorter sentences. So elements of discourse which were in one sentence in French were occasionally split over two sentences in German or English, and thus an entity transition was over two consecutive sentences in French, but had a sentence between them in the other two languages. As a result, the XXX transition count was typically higher for French. Interestingly, French also exhibited a higher count of $XX-$ transitions, often over sentences 1 and 2. Of course, we can enforce the constraint of strictly parallel sentences, but it is interesting to see the natural linguistic variation.

6.2 Linguistic trends

Interestingly, another reason for the variation across languages may be the fact that in French there is a tendency to use a noun in the plural as well as singular. For example, in document 37 of the **LIG** corpus the French used 2 separate entities where the English had one: 'inequality', which occurred at positions: 0, 1, 2, 3, 4, 12, 13, 14, 17, 18, 19, 21, 31, was rendered in French by 2 separate entities: 'inégalités' at 0, 1, 2, 4, 12, 14, 17, 18, 19, 31 'l'inégalité' at 2, 3, 13.

This phenomenon occurred elsewhere too: 'effort' in English occurred in the following sentences of document 24: 8, 9, 10, 11. In French we actually find 3 separate entities used, due to the way the parser dealt with the definite article: 'l'effort' at 8, 'effort' at 9, 11 and 'efforts' at 9, 10. While we can adapt our models (via lemmatisation) to account for the linguistic variation, it is important that we appreciate the linguistic variation in the first place, if we are to ensure appropriate lexical coherence.

In addition, sometimes an entity in English is actually rendered as an adjective in French, and therefore not tracked in the grid, such as document 5, where the source text, i.e. French, has 'crises cambiaires' rendered in the English as 'currency crises', and while 'currency' is identified as an entity in English, it is an adjective in French, thus not identified as an entity. Apart from affecting the transition probabilities, it would seem that some form of lexical chains is necessary to fully capture all the necessary lexical information in this multilingual setting. In the same document, 'currency' occurs 8 times as an entity in the English, yet in the French besides being rendered as an adjective twice, is rendered 4 times as 'caisse d'émission' and only once as 'monnaie'. This is reflected in the fact that for this document the English had 127 entities where the French had 152.

Another interesting point to note is that in general German exhibited a higher entity count. This is to be expected, as German is more nominal in structure than, for example, French. This count is also affected by the amount of compound verbs in German, and how we decide to model them. Thus, for example, from a document on cars, the word 'car' features as a main entity, but whereas it appears 4 and 6 times in French ['voiture' at sentences 6, 8, 23, 31, 32, 33] and English ['car' at sentences 5, 7, 22, 31, 32, 33] respectively, in German it only appears twice ['Auto' at sentences 7, 22]. However, 'car' is part of a collection of compound

7 Examining lexical coherence in a multilingual setting

words in German, such as 'High-end-auto' at sentence 31 in the document, [31=X] and 'Luxusauto' at sentence [32=X]. As it occurs in a different form, it is, in this instance, tracked as a different entity altogether.

Similarly, German exhibited a high ratio of $X - X$ transitions, where an entity skips a sentence, then reoccurs. This is explained by the occurrence of more, shorter sentences, as described above, and also by the compounding factor. With shorter sentences there is a greater chance that entities are split between two sentences, where the French may have had one. This also leads to lower likelihood of a transition to the next sentence; the transition would instead skip one sentence (appear as $X - X$ transition instead of $XX-$ or XXX). Plus a particular entity may not appear in three consecutive sentences, as it may have done in the French or English versions, because in the middle sentence it is part of a compound verb.

This illustrates the linguistic differences that need to be taken into account when examining comparative coherence in a multilingual context. This could lead to a decision to lemmatise before extracting grids or graphs, but in that case they are no longer strictly **entity** grids. We can apply linguistic processing to make the different grids comparable, but that should be sensitive to the linguistic variation, as overly processing to make them comparable will lose the natural expression in a particular language.

6.3 Source language implications

In some cases the quality of the text was also an issue. WMT data (from which the **LIG** corpus was also derived) is generated both from texts originally in a given language, e.g. English, and texts manually translated from other languages (e.g. Czech) into that language (say English). And in some cases the human translation of the documents was not particularly good. This was the case for some of the English documents translated from Czech in the **newstest2008** corpus. This has a direct influence on the coherence of the text, yet as noted by Cartoni et al. (2011), often those using this WMT corpus fail to realise the significance of whether a text is an original or a translation.

What also has to be taken into account is the language of the source text, and the tendency for it to affect the target text in style, depending on how literal the translation is.

6.4 Entity realisations

It is interesting to trace how the main entities in a given text are realised across the languages. See Table 3 where each numbered column represents a sentence in that parallel document. We have cut the last few sentences from the table, in order to fit it in.

Table 3: Occurrences of 'Brown' in various sentences of parallel document (dropping last sentences of document due to spacing)

	0	1	2	3	4	5	6	7	8	9	10	11	12	13	14	15	16	17
DE	x	-	-	x	x	x	-	-	-	-	-	x	-	-	-	x	-	x
FR	x	-	-	x	x	x	-	-	-	-	-	x	-	-	-	x	-	x
EN	x	-	x	-	x	-	-	-	-	x	-	-	-	-	x	-	x	-
	18	19	20	21	22	23	24	25	26	27	28	29	30	31	32	33	34	35
DE	-	x	-	x	-	-	-	-	-	x	-	-	-	-	x	x	-	-
FR	-	x	-	-	x	-	-	-	-	-	x	-	-	-	-	x	x	-
EN	x	-	-	x	-	-	-	-	-	x	-	-	-	-	-	x	-	-

We can clearly see how the main subject is realised through the document, albeit not at identical positions. On occasion, this is affected by differences in sentence breaks. In this case the French and German entities were closely matched in position at the start of the document, and then the English and German by the end. However, the point is that in general, there are the same number of occurrences, as the thread of discourse is traced through each document with exact positions dependent on sentence breaks. This pattern of occurrences is valuable information which among other things can potentially be used to improve anaphora resolution in the target text. Centering Theory has been used (Kehler 1997) to resolve referents by working out the backward looking centre for a sentence. Thus one of the entities referred to in one sentence may well be referred to in a subsequent sentence by a reference (Clarke & Lapata 2010). This study in entity grids has the potential to be useful in this domain too.

7 Multilingual graphs

7.1 Compound splitting

We also analyse the graph framework in a multilingual setting to try and garner additional insight into variations in coherence patterns in different languages. The intuition is that this framework could be more informative than the grid as it spans connections between not just adjacent sentences, but any subsequent ones.

Our initial experiments take all nouns in the document as discourse entities, as recommended by Elsner & Charniak (2011), and investigate how the projections are realised by lexical items. As discovered during experiments for the entity grid, the entity spread over sentences may vary from language to language (more on this below).

We used the weighted projection, which considers the frequencies of the various entities in the documents, which we determined was more appropriate than syntax in a comparative multilingual context. As regards incorporating syntax for other models, Strube & Hahn (1999) suggests that for freer word-order languages, "We claim that grammatical role criteria should be replaced by criteria that reflect the functional information structure of the utterances". This is particularly relevant for German. Our intuition is that the weighted projection gives the best appreciation of the cohesive links between sentences, as it gives a higher weighting where they are more frequent, unlike the unweighted one which simply logs the sentences which an entity occurs in.

We used the same WMT dataset as for the grid experiments. The graph coherence scores were computed for all parallel multilingual documents and results are displayed in Table 4.

Table 4: Number of documents (out of 90) for a given language which scored the highest among the 3 languages

	coherence score	coherence score without compound splitter
French	26	30
English	47	56
German	17	4

On closer analysis we encountered the same issue with German compounds as for the grid, whereby the entities in the German grid were more sparse, and more discontinuous in nature, due to the fact that compound words accounted for several entities. To establish just how much difference this was making, we also tried applying a compound splitter for German[3]. So for a given entity, we check if it decomposes into several entities, and if so each is entered separately in the graph. This resulted in a more uniform coherence score over the 3 languages. Whereas German had the highest coherence score for only 4 out of the 90 documents when no compound splitter was applied, this figure rose to 17 with a compound splitter. This is perhaps more meaningful when doing crosslingual comparisons.

---

[3] http://www.danielnaber.de/jwordsplitter, Licensed under the Apache License

7.2 Crosslingual similarity

Interestingly, looking at the coherence scores for all 3 languages, they exhibit remarkably similar graph profiles (Figure 2). As in the documents which result in a low score for English are similarly low for French and German. So it would seem that it is possible to assess lexical coherence as judged by this metric in a crosslingual manner, albeit as one aspect of coherence, not as sufficient to alone judge the overall coherence of the document. As Tanskanen (2006) point out, "cohesion may not work in absolutely identical ways in all languages, but the strategies of forming cohesive relations seem to display considerable similarity across languages".

The English documents had the largest proportion of high coherence scores, scoring highest more often than French or German. This could be a general characteristic that English involves more coherence as expressed via simple entity-based coherence and that in German coherence is possibly achieved through other means. Lapshinova-Koltunski (2015a) illustrate, that languages tend to vary in the way they use discourse features.

It certainly supports our findings in the grid experiments, where English had the highest number of entity transitions. From this it would seem that out of these three languages, German exhibits the least entity based coherence, while the highest scores are exhibited by English, followed by French. As Wong & Kit (2012) note, the lexical cohesion devices have to not only be recognised, but used appropriately. And this may differ from the source text to the target text.

7.3 Source language implications

As mentioned already, it is important for this data set to realise what the source language is, and this is marked up on the documents within the WMT data set. This is relevant because it indicates which languages are original texts and which are translations. The first 30 documents are originally Hungarian and Czech (so documents 0-29 in our code). The subsequent 15 ones are originally French (docs 30-44), the next 15 are Spanish (45-59), the next 15 are English (60-74) then German (75-90). This is interesting, as we can then see patterns emerging of naturally coherent texts. It also means that for a number of documents, our French, German and English versions are all translations. One point to note is that ideally this should be extended over an additional corpus, to gain more data, as otherwise we just have 15 texts of each original language. In the meantime, we can see from Table 5 how these affect the scores assigned under this metric. While it is tempting to consider whether having an original German text means that the

7 Examining lexical coherence in a multilingual setting

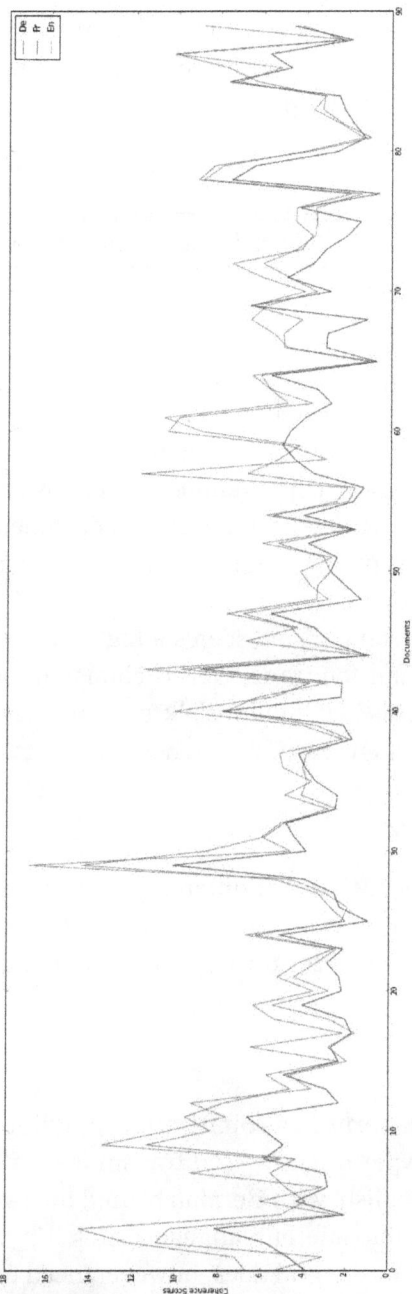

Figure 2: Multilingual graph coherence scores, displaying the score (y-axis) for each document (x-axis)

coherence is higher for German and more evenly scoring in general, or whether an English source text results in less coherence for the German, the number of documents in this preliminary work are not representative enough. This could be worthwhile pursuing as a corpus study, however.

Table 5: Breakdown of highest scoring documents

	French highest	English highest	German highest
French original (docs 30-44)	3	8	4
English original (docs 60-74)	6	8	1
German original (docs 75-90)	4	6	5

Although the projection score is normalised in that the sum of projections is multiplied by 1/N where N is the number of sentences, there is an inevitable bias in favour of longer documents, for example, document 65 in our experiment using the WMT data has only 3 sentences, and reads as a coherent one, yet due to the shortness has a low score.

Yet document 29, by comparison, scores a high score yet reads incoherently - it is originally Czech, and the translation is clumsy in parts. The high score is due to repetition of words like 'millions', 'krona' or 'year' or their equivalent in French and German. French scores the highest, but seems to also be poor quality.

7.4 Lexical coherence

Intuitively, it would seem that this different perspective, i.e. the graph model, offers more insight into crosslingual coherence patterns, in that it captures all the connections between entities throughout the entire document.

8 Conclusions

We observed distinct patterns in a comparative multilingual approach: the probabilities for different types of entity grid transitions varied, and were generally lower in French than English, with German behind the two, indicating a different coherence structure in the different languages.

The standard format of the grid does, however, need to be modified for a multilingual context. It is clear that there are divergences between languages, as regards entity based coherence. As before, French will still have multiple representations for what would potentially be one entity in English: the use of singular and plural forms of the noun as noticed in French, or adjectival forms representing the entity. We have also detected differences in implementation due to the compound structure of German; in German while compound nouns affect the coherence score considerably, even with a compound splitter (as for the graph) the coherence score is still generally lower. Possible extensions to this research include expanding the grid to include lexical chains, in place of simple entities, or incorporating a vector of similar terms which would potentially take account of these issues and allow for crosslingual variance in the semantic coverage of an individual lexical item. This would potentially better account for the compound structure of German, and the use of singular and plural forms of the noun as noticed in French, or adjectival forms representing the entity. It is valuable to register and identify the differences and bear them in mind for future development, particularly for crosslingual transfer.

We have seen that the graph leads to a clear picture of entity-based coherence scores. This is perhaps more useful than the grid for comparative studies. We can also see better how entity-based coherence is achieved in different languages. Here the exact sentence breaks do not matter so much, and the score is based on how cohesive the document is as a whole. In future research we will note the significance of whether a text is an original or a translation, filtering our data based on the original language.

Our next step will be to use the graph metric as part of the reranking process within an MT system, to try and assess its ability to disambiguate entities.

The challenge from an MT point of view would be to ensure that the correspondences are maintained, so an entity chain is carried over from source to target text, despite differences in syntax and sentence structure. However, this is insufficient to ensure that the document is fully coherent – more linguistically based elements are necessary to do that.

References

Barzilay, Regina & Mirella Lapata. 2005. Modeling local coherence: An Entity-Based approach. In *Proceedings of the 43rd Annual Meeting of the Association for Computational Linguistics (ACL'05)*, 141–148. Ann Arbor, Michigan. http://www.aclweb.org/anthology/P05-1018. DOI:10.3115/1219840.1219858

Barzilay, Regina & Mirella Lapata. 2008. Modeling local coherence: An entity-based approach. *Computational Linguistics* 34(1). 1–34. DOI:10.1162/coli.2008.34.1.1

Burstein, Jill, Joel R. Tetreault & Slava Andreyev. 2010. Using Entity-Based features to model coherence in student essays. In *Proceedings of HLT-NAACL*, 681–684.

Carpuat, Marine & Michel Simard. 2012. The trouble with SMT consistency. In *Proceedings of WMT*, 442–449. Montreal, Canada.

Cartoni, Bruno, Sandrine Zufferey, Thomas Meyer & Andrei Popescu-Belis. 2011. How comparable are parallel corpora? Measuring the distribution of general vocabulary and connectives. In *Proceedings of the 4th Workshop on Building and Using Comparable Corpora: Comparable Corpora and the Web* (BUCC '11), 78–86. Stroudsburg, PA, USA: Association for Computational Linguistics.

Cheung, Jackie Chi Kit & Gerald Penn. 2010. Entity-based local coherence modelling using topological fields. In *ACL*, 186–195. http://www.aclweb.org/anthology/P10-1020.

Clarke, James & Mirella Lapata. 2010. Discourse constraints for document compression. *Computational Linguistics* 36(3). 411–441.

Elsner, Micha, Joseph Austerweil & Eugene Charniak. 2007. A unified local and global model for discourse coherence. In *Proceedings of HLT-NAACL*, 436–443.

Elsner, Micha & Eugene Charniak. 2011. Extending the entity grid with Entity-Specific features. In *Proceedings of ACL*, 125–129.

Filippova, Katja & Michael Strube. 2007. Extending the entity-grid coherence model to semantically related entities. In *Proceedings of the 11th European Workshop on Natural Language Generation* (ENLG '07), 139–142. Stroudsburg, PA, USA: Association for Computational Linguistics. http://dl.acm.org/citation.cfm?id=1610163.1610187.

Grosz, Barbara J. & Candace L. Sidner. 1986. Attention, intentions, and the structure of discourse. *Computational Linguistics* 12(3). 175–204. http://dl.acm.org/citation.cfm?id=12457.12458.

Grosz, Barbara J., Scott Weinstein & Aravind K. Joshi. 1995. Centering: A framework for modeling the local coherence of discourse. *Computational Linguistics* 21. 203–225.

Guinaudeau, Camille & Michael Strube. 2013. Graph-based local coherence modeling. In *Proceedings of ACL*, 93–103.

Hardmeier, Christian. 2012. Discourse in statistical machine translation. *Discours* (11).

Kehler, Andrew. 1997. Current theories of centering for pronoun interpretation: A critical evaluation. *Computational Linguistics* 23(3). 467–475.

Lapata, Mirella. 2005. Automatic evaluation of text coherence: Models and representations. In *Proceedings of IJCAI*, 1085–1090.

Lapshinova-Koltunski, Ekaterina. 2015a. Exploration of inter- and intralingual variation of discourse phenomena. In *Proceedings of the 2nd Workshop on Discourse in Machine Translation*, 158–167. Lisbon, Portugal.

Lapshinova-Koltunski, Ekaterina. 2015b. Variation in translation: Evidence from corpora. In Claudio Fantinuoli & Federico Zanettin (eds.), *New directions in corpus-based translation studies* (Translation and Multilingual Natural Language Processing), 93–113. Berlin: Language Science Press.

Potet, Marion, Emmanuelle Esperança-Rodier, Laurent Besacier & Hervé Blanchon. 2012. *Collection of a Large Database of French-English SMT Output Corrections*.

Strube, Michael & Udo Hahn. 1999. Functional centering: Grounding referential coherence in information structure. *Computational Linguistics* 25(3). 309–344. http://dl.acm.org/citation.cfm?id=973321.973328.

Tanskanen, Sanna-Kaisa. 2006. *Collaborating towards coherence: Lexical cohesion in English discourse* (Pragmatics & Beyond New Series). Amsterdam: John Benjamins Publishing Company.

Tiedemann, Jörg. 2010. Context adaptation in statistical machine translation using models with exponentially decaying cache. In *Proceedings of the 2010 Workshop on Domain Adaptation for Natural Language Processing*, 8–15. Uppsala, Sweden.

Wong, Billy Tak-Ming & Chunyu Kit. 2012. Extending machine translation evaluation metrics with lexical cohesion to document level. In *Proceedings of EMNLP-CoNLL*, 1060–1068.

Xiong, Deyi, Yang Ding, Min Zhang & Chew Lim Tan. 2013a. Lexical chain based cohesion models for Document-Level statistical machine translation. In *Proceedings of EMNLP*, 1563–1573.

Xiong, Deyi, Guosheng Ben, Min Zhang, Yajuan Lv & Qun Liu. 2013b. Modeling lexical cohesion for Document-Level machine translation. In *Proceedings of IJCAI*.

Name index

Aijmer, Karin, 13
Alekseyenko, Nataliya V., 82
Andreyev, Slava, 134
Argamon, Shlomo, 77
Ariel, Mira, 36
Arlin, Nathalie, 52
Arnovick, Leslie, 16
Auger, Alain, 60
Austerweil, Joseph, 134

Baayen, R. Harald, 118
Bae, Hee Sook, 58
Baker, Mona, 78, 81, 105, 111
Baroni, Marco, 77, 81, 89
Barrière, Caroline, 60
Barzilay, Regina, 133–135, 137
Bauer, Jaroslav, 15
Becher, Viktor, 110, 111
Behrens, Bergljot, 78
Bejček, Eduard, 36
Bernardini, Silvia, 77, 80, 81, 89
Bisiada, Mario, 110, 111
Blum-Kulka, Shoshana, 78, 110
Bowker, Lynne, 52
Breiman, Leo, 87
Brinker, Klaus, 1
Budanitsky, Alexander, 60
Bührig, Kristin, 109
Burstein, Jill, 134

Cabrè, Maria Teresa, 50
Carpuat, Marine, 110, 112, 132, 133

Carreño Cruz, Sahara Iveth, 50
Carston, Robyn, 78
Cartoni, Bruno, 141
Castagnoli, Sara, 81
Cea, Guadalupe Aguado-de, 52
Chambers, John M., 117
Charniak, Eugene, 134, 135, 142
Chesterman, Andrew, 80
Cheung, Jackie Chi Kit, 137
Chiarcos, Christian, 36
Ciapuscio, Guiomar E., 58
Claridge, Claudia, 16
Clarke, James, 142
Collet, Tanja, 50, 53
Cuenca, Maria-Josep, 14

Dai, Guangrong, 80
Daille, Béatrice, 51, 52
Darbelnet, Jean, 110
Degand, Liesbeth, 16
Depierre, Amélie, 52
Deshors, Sandra C., 77, 82, 87, 89, 90
Dipper, Stefanie, 109, 110
Doherty, Monica, 111

Eckert, Miriam, 35
Eggins, Suzanne, 69
Elsner, Micha, 134, 135, 142
Evers-Vermeul, Jacqueline, 16
Evert, Stefan, 9, 114

Fabricius-Hansen, Cathrine, 77, 111

Name index

Fernández Silva, Sabela, 50, 52
Filippova, Katja, 137
Fischer, Kerstin, 13
Fraser, Bruce, 13
Freixa, Judit, 50

Gellerstam, Martin, 106, 111
Geyken, Alexander, 18
Gile, Daniel, 77
Gómez, Adelina, 70
Gómez-González, María de los Ángeles, 109
González-Jover, 70
Graesser, Arthur C., 2
Granger, Sylviane, 80
Grenoble, Lenore A., 78
Grepl, Miroslav, 25
Gries, Stefan Th., 77, 82, 87, 89, 90
Grosz, Barbara J., 36, 133, 134
Guillou, Liane, 112
Guinaudeau, Camille, 134–136
Guzmán, Alexandria E., 78, 79

Hahn, Udo, 143
Hajičová, Eva, 14, 35–38
Hajlaoui, Najeh, 106
Hakulinen, Auli, 13
Hall, Mark, 86, 87
Halliday, Michael A. K., 2, 29, 53, 107–109
Hansen, Maj-Britt Mosegaard, 13
Hansen-Schirra, Silvia, 80, 81, 105, 113, 124
Hardmeier, Christian, 106, 112, 132, 133
Harper, Douglas, 18
Hasan, Ruqaiya, 2, 29, 53, 107–109
Hatim, Basil, 77, 78
Hawkins, Shane, 52

He, Lianzhen, 80
Heylen, Kris, 60
Hinkel, Eli, 77
Hirst, Graeme, 60
Hladká, Barbora, 35
Holub, Josef, 15
House, Juliane, 109

Joshi, Aravind K., 13, 28, 29, 36, 133, 134

Kachroo, Balkrishan, 77
Kazama, Jun'ichi, 60
Kehler, Andrew, 142
Kerremans, Koen, 50, 54
Kilgarriff, Adam, 60
Kiss, Tibor, 83
Kit, Chunyu, 132, 133, 144
Klein, Wolfgang, 18
Klin, Celia M., 78, 79
Komen, Erwin R., 36
Kopečný, František, 15
Koppel, Moshe, 77
Krifka, Manfred, 2
Kučová, Lucie, 35
Kunilovskaya, Maria, 76, 77, 81, 83, 95
Kunz, Kerstin, 108–111, 118, 120, 121
Kutuzov, Andrey, 76, 77, 81–83, 95
Kuzmenko, Elizaveta, 82

L'Homme, Marie-Claude, 58
Lambrecht, Knud, 2
Lapata, Mirella, 133–135, 137, 142
Lapshinova-Koltunski, Ekaterina, 105, 106, 108, 109, 111–113, 121, 126, 139, 144
Laviosa, Sara, 80
Laviosa-Braithwaite, Sara, 111

Name index

Lenker, Ursula, 18
Li, Junyi Jessy, 110, 112
Louwerse, Max M., 2

Marcu, Daniel, 60
Martin, James R., 29
Mascarell, Laura, 112
Maschler, Yael, 13
Mason, Ian, 77, 78
Matthiessen, Christian, 2, 108, 109
Meurman-Solin, Anneli, 18
Meyer, Thomas, 79, 106, 110, 112
Mikhailov, Mikhail, 82
Mírovský, Jiří, 24
Montiel-Ponsoda, Elena, 52

Nedoluzhko, Anna, 36, 38, 39
Nenkova, Ani, 110, 112
Neumann, Arne, 36
Neumann, Stella, 105, 113, 124

Olohan, Maeve, 80

Pajas, Petr, 8, 39, 80
Partee, Barbara, 14, 37, 38
Pastor, G. Corpas, 77, 80, 81
Peirsman, Yves, 60
Penn, Gerald, 137
Poláková, Lucie, 28
Popescu-Belis, Andrei, 79, 106
Potet, Marion, 136
Prasad, Rashmi, 13, 14, 28, 29

Quinlan, J. Ross, 87

Ramm, Wiebke, 77
Rayson, Paul, 80
Rejzek, Jiří, 15
Resche, Catherine, 52
Rogers, Margaret, 54

Rychlý, Pavel, 60
Rysová, Kateřina, 13, 14, 23, 24, 27, 28, 36, 38
Rysová, Magdaléna, 14, 23–25, 27, 28, 36, 38

Schiffrin, Deborah, 13
Schmid, Helmut, 113
Schourup, Lawrence, 13
Segalovich, Ilya, 84
Seiss, Melanie, 109, 110
Sgall, Petr, 14, 37, 38
Shimizu, Nobuyuki, 60
Shimoni, Anat Rachel, 77
Shloush, Shelley, 13
Sidner, Candace L., 36, 133
Simard, Michel, 132, 133
Solfjeld, Kåre, 77
Speelman, Dirk, 60
Stede, Manfred, 36
Steiner, Erich, 105, 113, 124
Štěpánek, Jan, 8, 39, 80
Strube, Michael, 35, 134–137, 143
Strunk, Jan, 83

Taboada, Maite, 109
Tanskanen, Sanna-Kaisa, 53, 54, 144
Teich, Elke, 105, 110
Temmerman, Rita, 50, 52
Tetreault, Joel R., 134
Tiedemann, Jörg, 132, 133

Unger, Christoph, 78
Urgelles-Coll, Miriam, 13

van Dijk, Teun A., 78
van Halteren, Hans, 77
Vandenbergen, Anne-Marie Simon, 16

Name index

Vinay, Jean P., 110

Webber, Bonnie, 13, 28, 29, 106, 110, 112
Weeds, Julie, 60
Weinstein, Scott, 36, 133, 134
Widdowson, H. G., 2
Wong, Billy Tak-Ming, 132, 133, 144

Xiao, Richard, 80
Xiong, Deyi, 132, 133

Yue, Ming, 80

Zanettin, Federico, 80
Zinsmeister, Heike, 109, 110
Zwicky, Arnold M., 13

Subject index

anaphora, 14, 35, 109, 112, 142
annotation of sentence information structure, 7, 14, 36, 37, 38^3, 46

boundary class, 84, 85, 87–89

changement climatique, 71
classifier, 84, 87, 89, 99
cluster label, 8, 56, 58, 61, 63, 69
coherence, 1–9, 26, 35, 36, 36^1, 44, 53, 77, 79, 106, 107, 109, 119, 131–138, 140–144, 146, 147
cohesion, 1–4, 7, 9, 51, 53, 77–79, 82, 105, 109, 111–113, 121, 132, 133, 144
collocation, 53, 54
compound, 16, 137, 138, 140, 141, 143, 147
compound splitter, 143, 147
connective formation, 12, 18, 20, 22, 25
consistency, 8, 61, 66, 70, 112, 133
contextual boundness, 7, 36–38
coreference, 2, 4, 7, 8, 14, 35–40, 42, 44–46, 106, 108–110, 112, 114, 122
coreference arrow, 39
coreference relation, 39
coreferential analysis, 50–52, 54, 56, 60, 61, 68, 70
coreferential chain, 54, 65, 67

correlation, 45, 68, 90, 92, 96, 117
current sentence, 79, 84, 86
current token, 84–87, 91, 92, 99
Czech, 5, 12–14, 14^1, 15, 15^2, 15^3, 16–18, 18^4, 18^5, 20–26, 30, 31, 36, 37, 46, 141, 144, 146

demonstrative pronoun, 17, 18, 21–23, 25, 109
dependency, 40, 98
detection, 11, 14, 76, 88, 89
discourse marker, 85–87, 94, 95
discourse relation, 12, 26, 27, 29

EEA, 55, 68
entity grid, 134–137, 143, 146
entity transition, 9, 135, 137–139
evaluation, 8, 83, 86, 109, 111, 126, 133, 134
experiment, 81, 96, 113, 135, 137, 146
explicit discourse, 7, 14, 28
explicitation, 80, 111, 112, 119, 123, 126
expressing identity, 120, 123
extraction, 71, 114, 116

feature selection, 8, 79, 85, 90
first token, 85–87, 93
French, 4, 6, 50, 54–56, 60, 64–66, 66^4, 67, 68, 71, 83, 132, 136–144, 146, 147

genre, 134, 138

Subject index

German, 4–6, 12, 15, 15^2, 16, 18, 18^4, 18^6, 20, 22, 31, 54, 106, 107, 109–114, 118, 121, 122, 125, 126, 136–144, 146, 147
grammaticalization, 3, 5, 7, 12, 16, 18, 22–25, 30
GRE, 56, 68

historical origin, 5, 12, 14–16, 31

individual node, 44
information gain, 85, 91
information structure, 2–6, 39, 40, 78, 143
interaction, 3, 4, 35, 36, 39
interference, 78, 80, 82, 93, 96
interlingual variation, 50, 55, 56, 64

learner, 5, 6, 8, 76–78, 88, 91, 95–99
lexical chain, 56, 65
LIG, 6
logical flow, 1, 2, 107

machine translation, 1–5, 7–10, 76, 79, 97, 106, 107, 111, 112, 119, 124, 126
modifier, 115, 116, 119, 122
monolingual setting, 8, 133, 134
multilingual context, 8, 131, 132, 137, 141, 143, 146
multilingual corpus, 6, 8, 10, 107
multilingual setting, 9, 132, 134, 140, 142
multiword, 7, 12–16, 18, 20, 21, 24, 25, 27, 28, 30, 59, 62, 66^4, 98

navzdory této, 25–27
network, 51, 60, 69
new term, 61, 63
noise, 89, 91, 98

non-bound sentence, 8, 37, 40, 42, 45
non-bound sentence item, 42, 44, 45
non-connective, 27^{12}
normalisation, 80, 82, 95, 126

overall cohesiveness, 117, 118, 126

parallel corpus, 4, 6, 8, 9, 80–82, 113
part-of-speech, 9, 13, 23, 24, 107, 113, 114
PDTB, 28, 29
PoS, 77, 78, 81, 82, 85, 86, 92–94
previous context, 22, 36, 38, 39, 46

reference corpus, 8, 76, 77, 79, 91, 93, 98
referential expression, 58
register, 27^{11}, 52, 82, 110, 112, 113, 147
Russian, 4, 6, 8, 76–78, 82–84, 84^3, 87–90, 92–94, 96–99

segment, 36, 61, 63
semi-automated process, 63, 64
semi-automatic method, 8, 51, 60, 62
sentence boundary, 82, 84, 85, 89, 91–94, 96, 97, 99
sentence information structure, 7, 14^1, 35–37, 44, 45
sentence item, 42–46
sentence length, 77, 78, 81, 84, 86, 87, 91, 95, 96
sequence, 65, 93, 96, 137
significance analysis, 81, 95
source language, 50, 51, 56, 60, 64, 67, 69, 70, 80, 110, 144
source text, 2, 50, 61, 64, 95, 97, 111, 133, 140, 141, 144, 146
standard language, 8, 79, 93, 96
study of terminological variation, 51, 52

Subject index

subordinate conjunction, 85, 95
syntactic translationese, 76, 78, 98

target language, 7, 50, 61, 67, 70, 77, 78, 106, 107, 111, 113, 125, 126
target text, 2, 56, 111, 133, 134, 141, 142, 144, 147
term candidate, 58, 59, 61–63
term variant, 59, 61, 63
terminological variation, 50–54, 60
terminology, 8, 29, 30, 50, 51, 53, 54, 58, 133
text coreference arrow, 39, 43–45
text coreference connection, 39, 43
text coreference relation, 45
text fluency, 81
text sample, 56, 58
textual perspective, 50–53
transition profile, 65
translation corpus, 84, 88, 90–93
translation quality, 6, 8, 79, 131
translationese, 2, 77, 79–83, 95, 97, 99, 107, 111, 120
Treebank, 3, 5, 7, 12, 13, 20, 27, 28, 31, 36, 37, 45
TTR, 121, 122, 124

usage, 21, 28, 83, 89, 96, 110, 112, 126

variety, 8, 76, 83, 90, 93, 108, 116
visualisation, 9, 68, 69, 116, 117

WMT, 6, 136, 137, 139, 141, 143, 144, 146

Did you like this book?

This book was brought to you for free

Please help us in providing free access to linguistic research worldwide. Visit http://www.langsci-press.org/donate to provide financial support or register as a community proofreader or typesetter at http://www.langsci-press.org/register.

language science press

www.ingramcontent.com/pod-product-compliance
Lightning Source LLC
Chambersburg PA
CBHW080603170426
43196CB00017B/2889